D0661929

Experiments in Artificial Intelligence for Small Computers

by John Krutch

Howard W. Sams & Co., Inc.
4300 WEST 62ND ST. INDIANAPOLIS, INDIANA 46268 USA

International Standard Book Number: 0-672-21785-6
Library of Congress Catalog Card Number: 80-53270

Printed in the United States of America.

Preface

Most people are fascinated by the subject of artificial intelligence, or AI. The idea of a computer, a mere box of parts, which demonstrates abilities that we have always considered to be solely and uniquely human, is staggering to most of us. And the concept becomes even more shattering, more destructive to our self-esteem, when we consider that many computer scientists believe that computers may eventually be able not only to match human intellectual capacities, but far outstrip them.

The concept of intelligent computers evokes strong responses. Some people find the idea interesting and challenging. Others find it horrifying. But whatever one's feelings may be in regard to artificial intelligence, it is impossible to deny that researchers in this field have made enormous strides in recent years.

Let's consider just one example. Fifteen years ago, chess-playing programs were so weak that they could be trounced without much effort by weak amateurs. Today, chess programs have evolved to the point where the best of them can beat or give stiff competition to professional players. One such program, Northwestern University's CHESS 4.7, has beaten International Master David Levy in a tournament game, and professional players such as George Koltanowski are predicting that soon computers will be regularly competing against grandmasters in tournament play. The current version of the Northwestern CHESS is an expert with a USCF rating of about 2050.

Furthermore, we may be closer to artificial intelligence than some people think. At least one AI researcher—Philip C. Jackson of Xerox Corp.—is recommending that computer scientists, when working on certain types of AI programs, take certain precautions lest the program suddenly become intelligent and get out of control!

In the following chapters we will be exploring various fields of artificial intelligence. Problem-solving, creativity, communication with computers in "plain English"—all of these are covered. The only prerequisites are a computer with some form of extended BASIC, and some knowledge of BASIC on your part.

The emphasis in this book is on the *practical*. The book is intended so that you, the reader, can *experiment with* some of the techniques of artificial intelligence, not just read about them. While theory is not completely neglected, we avoid delving too deeply into theoretical matters.

The programs are all written in what is probably the most widely used form of microcomputer BASIC at the present time, namely, Microsoft's Level II BASIC for the Radio Shack TRS-80. The programs will run without alteration on any Level II or Disk BASIC-equipped TRS-80. They will run with minor alterations under other versions of Microsoft BASIC, e.g., Applesoft, PET BASIC, Exidy Sorcerer BASIC, etc. In addition, with a bit of effort most of the programs can be converted to BASIC dialects other than Microsoft, such as Texas Instruments* and Southwest Technical BASIC. An appendix is provided at the back of the book to assist you in such conversions.

BASIC is by no means an ideal language for artificial intelligence projects. But until more appropriate languages, such as LISP, become generally available for microcomputers, BASIC will remain the language of choice simply because of its wide popularity. The limitations of BASIC force certain limitations on the types of programs that can be written. But even within these limitations amazing things can be accomplished, as we shall see.

John Krutch

---

*TI 99/4 BASIC was written by Microsoft, but to TI specifications.

Contents

CHAPTER 7

APPENDIX

CHAPTER 1

Artificial Intelligence and BASIC

What is artificial intelligence concerned with? The main goal of artificial intelligence (AI) *is to make computers smarter.* Researchers in AI write programs which attempt to do tasks which ordinarily could be carried out only by a thinking, reasoning, human being. While no researcher has yet managed to discover a program which even comes close to transforming a computer into an intelligent entity, some of AI's most successful efforts are extraordinary and dazzle the mind with their possibilities.

We will be examining some of these programs in later chapters, but first let's look at an example a bit closer to home. Consider the following simple BASIC program:

```
10 X = RND(1000)
20 PRINT "SQUARE ROOT OF" X "IS" SQR(X)
30 GOTO 10
```

The program randomly selects a number between 1 and 1000, finds its square root and prints it, and repeats the process. This and other mathematical computations, some of them far more complex, can be and are executed every minute of every day by computers around the world. Furthermore, computers can make these calculations in a fraction of the time it would take even the most skilled human operator to come up with an answer.

A complex mathematical calculation is the sort of thing, before the advent of computers, we would have said required *intelligence* to do. The same goes for nearly every other type of computer activity: computers today are handling various scientific, business, and industrial processes which, fifty years ago, we would have unequivocally said required intelligence to perform. So even the simplest computer program, such as the three-line BASIC program above, could be said to be a certain limited demonstration of artificial intelligence.

The Scope of AI

The term "artificial intelligence" embraces a number of varied topics. Let's look at some of them.

Natural-language processing attempts to make computers understand "natural languages," such as English. Natural-language processing got off to a slow start in the 1950s, when abortive attempts were made to program computers to automatically translate Russian to English, but in recent years researchers working in this area have made significant advances.

Problem solving is an important field. The BASIC program above, which finds square roots, is a problem-solving program but it is severely limited in that the only type of problem it can solve is square roots. If we want to find solutions for some other class of problems, we are forced to write another program, and another program for another set of problems, and so on. What we need is a *general* problem-solving program which is able to find solutions to many different types of problems; the program would only need to be given enough information to deduce the solution to the problem, if one exists. Such a program might be able to solve problems in physics, chemistry, astronomy, and other "exact" sciences. It would be able to find the solution to any chess problem, prove theorems of logic and mathematics, or do any of a wide variety of tasks.

Pattern-recognition is central to much work in artificial intelligence. A computer is frequently given an undigested mass of raw data, in which there may be certain patterns which the computer needs to understand in order to be able to process the data. For example, suppose a situation arises where a computer-controlled mechanical hand must distinguish between nuts, bolts, and screws on an assembly line (the computer "sees" by means of a tv camera). Just how to recognize the object in front of it as nut, bolt, or screw can be a difficult job for the computer.

Another branch of AI is *automatic programming*. This involves making computers write programs to specifications supplied by a computer operator. Such a computer could have as a subsidiary function the ability to test and debug programs written by a human programmer.

Problem Areas of AI Programming

In this book we will be primarily concerned with writing artificial intelligence programs in BASIC. So it will be useful for us to look at some of the difficulties which are commonly encountered when it comes to putting together programs in artificial intelligence.

The programmer is faced with three major problem areas. How well the programmer overcomes these problem areas, in the course of translating his or her ideas into a computer language, will determine in large part how "intelligent" the resulting program is. These problem areas are *representation, search,* and *range*.

The problem of *how to represent* complex data structures in a computer language is by no means a problem that is limited to artificial intelligence. However, representation can be a particularly thorny problem for AI researchers, since the structures and processes which they try to model inside the computer are often especially complex.

The problem of *search* is an acute one in AI. Frequently an AI program will try to solve a given task by generating a huge multitude of possible solutions to the task, testing each solution as it is generated to determine if it's the right one. This is analogous to the BASIC programmer who, after finding a bug in a program and having isolated it to a certain variable X, doesn't try to figure out what the proper value of X should be, but merely assigns different values to the variable until the program produces the desired result when executed. The trouble with this approach, when used in AI programs, is that the set of possible solutions can be so enormous that the computer cannot generate and test all of them in a reasonable period. Imagine a BASIC programmer who had to assign a million or more different values to X, one after another, until the right value was found! Game-playing programs are particularly vulnerable to the problem of search, since there may be an exponential number of possible moves which must be tested before the best move is found.

Finally, there is the problem of *range*. Most AI programs to date operate within certain narrow, well-defined limits. While they may perform very well within these limits, their utility is not high simply because of these limits. But when the range of the program is extended, in order to enable it to operate on more types of data and provide it with more functions and increased utility, there is usually a tradeoff: The program, though it can now perform a greater range of tasks, doesn't perform individual tasks as well as it did previously. In other words, in artificial intelligence work a program's range is often inversely proportional to its efficiency.

KINGMOVE

KINGMOVE is a short BASIC program which will help to illustrate some of the concepts discussed previously. Fig. 1-1 shows the video display of a computer running KINGMOVE. We will see how the problems of representation, search, and range apply to an actual program.

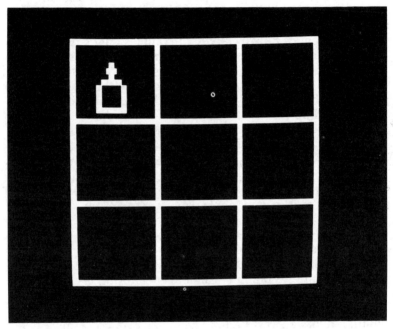

Fig. 1-1. Video display of computer running KINGMOVE.

In KINGMOVE a chess king is moved about on the small 3 × 3 chessboard shown in Fig. 1-2. Notice the square labelled "initial square"; the king always begins at this square. The program's job is to find the shortest path between the initial square and the square marked "goal square." The program is given the information that the shortest path will require exactly two moves. The program then proceeds to move the king along various paths across the board from the initial square to the goal square, over and over again, until it discovers the shortest path. The shortest path, of course, is 1 to 5 to 9.

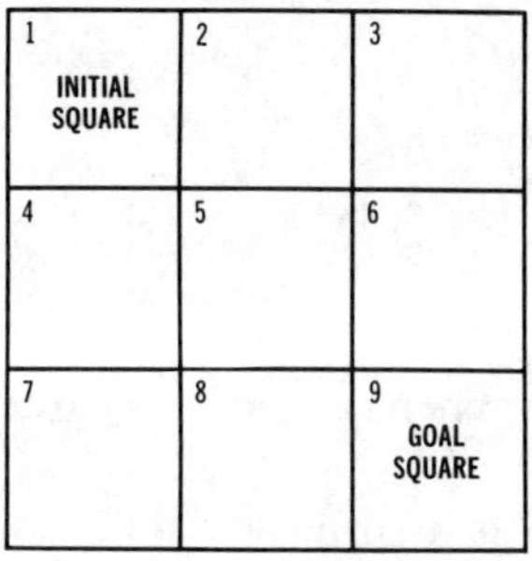

1 INITIAL SQUARE	2	3
4	5	6
7	8	9 GOAL SQUARE

Fig. 1-2. The program must find the shortest path between the initial square (1) and the goal square (9).

Structure of the Program

KINGMOVE, like all the programs in this book, is written in module-by-module fashion with a main routine, or *supervisor,* which calls the individual subroutines as they are needed. This makes the program far easier to understand than a similar program which doesn't employ this modular architecture. It also makes it easier to revise the program, since the prospective change can usually be made to just one subroutine, without need for revision in other parts of the program.

Here is the supervisor routine for KINGMOVE:

```
10 '          Supervisor
20 GOSUB 90    ' Initialization
30 GOSUB 150   ' Set array to initial piece arrangement
40 GOSUB 190   ' Draw board
50 GOSUB 410   ' Print current king position
60 GOSUB 290   ' King's move
70 GOSUB 410
80 GOTO 60
```

Notice that there are five subroutines, beginning at lines 90, 150, 190, 290, and 410. Three of them are executed just once, at the beginning of the program: the initialization subroutine, the subroutine that sets the array to the initial piece configuration, and the subroutine that draws the board. The remaining two subroutines, which generate the king's moves from one square to the next and handle the graphics routines involved, are executed repeatedly until the computer solves the problem.

Let's examine each of the five subroutines in turn.

Initialization Routines

Here is the initialization subroutine:

```
90 '          Initialization
100 CLS
110 RANDOM
120 CU = 1
130 K$ = CHR$(174) + CHR$(157) + STRING$(5, 32) + CHR$(26) +
    STRING$(12, 24) + STRING$(3, 32) + CHR$(188) +
    STRING$(4, 131) + CHR$(188) + CHR$(26) + STRING$(6, 24) +
    CHR$(191) + STRING$(4, 176) + CHR$(191)
140 E$ = STRING$(4, 8) + STRING$(10, 32) + CHR$(26) +
    STRING$(10, 8) + CHR$(26) + STRING$(10, 32)
145 RETURN
```

K$ is a string variable which contains the characters necessary to draw a chess king on the video display. Just how this is done, of course, depends in large part on the version of BASIC you are using. In this instance a combination of graphics characters and control characters, especially cursor control characters, is used. Whenever K$ is printed, the king is shown on the display.

The variable E$ ("E" stands for "empty") contains control characters which will erase a previously printed king from the display. This is necessary to keep the board up to date.

CU (for "current") stores a number from 1 to 9 which indicates the square the king is currently occupying. Since the king starts at square 1, CU is set to this value initially.

The next subroutine to be called by the supervisor sets array A$ to the initial piece arrangement:

```
150 '        Set array to initial piece arrangement
160 A$(1) = K$: A$(2) = E$: A$(3) = E$: A$(4) = E$: A$(5) = E$
170 A$(6) = E$: A$(7) = E$: A$(8) = E$: A$(9) = E$
180 RETURN
```

This subroutine solves the problem of representation in a simple manner. We let each of the nine squares of Fig. 1-2 be represented by one of the nine variables in the 1 × 9 array A$. Square 1 is represented by A$(1), square 2 by A$(2), and so on. To set the array to the beginning piece configuration, K$ is placed in A$(1), since A$(1) represents the initial square, and the king always starts from the initial square. Since the other eight squares are empty, E$ is placed into the corresponding array variables.

Representation of Data

Representation of a program's important data structures may have to be done twice in the same program. The reason is that the data structures may have to be accessed not only by the computer, but also, in many instances, by the person interacting with or monitoring the progress of the computer.

This is true of KINGMOVE. The array A$ represents the data in such a way that it can be understood by the computer. The subroutine at 190, which draws the board on the screen, as well as the subroutine at 410, which prints the current king position, represents the data in such a way that it can be understood by the person monitoring the program.

Both subroutines are graphics routines, so they will have to be redone, in part or entirety, for your BASIC.

Move Generation

The next subroutine generates the king's moves:

```
290 '          King's move
300 ST$ = "1"
310 R2 = RND(4): IF R2 = 2 THEN 310
320 IF R2 = 1 THEN IF CU = 3 OR CU = 6 THEN 310
330 IF R2 = 4 THEN IF CU = 3 OR CU = 7 THEN 310
340 IF CU + R2 > 9 THEN 310
350 OC = CU: CU = CU + R2
360 ST$ = ST$ + MID$(STR$(CU), 2, 1)
370 GOSUB 410
380 IF CU = 9 THEN OC = CU: CU = 1: ELSE 310
390 IF LEN(ST$) = 3 THEN PRINT @ 442, "SHORT-";: PRINT @ 506,
    "EST";: PRINT @ 570, "PATH:";: PRINT @ 634, ST$;: GOTO 390
400 RETURN
```

Lines 310 through 340 find a move with the help of the random number generator; if the result is an impossible move, new moves are generated until a valid move is found. Line 350 puts the current square number into CU; the previous current square number is assigned to OC.

A string which represents the squares the king has travelled over is built up by line 360. One string which might result is

12369

which means that the king has moved from the initial square to square 2 to square 3 to square 6 to the goal square.

As previously mentioned, KINGMOVE is given the highly important information that the path it is seeking is exactly two moves long. This data is imparted in line 390, where program execution stops if the length of the string is 3.

As you can see, this subroutine generates random paths along the chessboard for the king to follow, one after another, until the shortest path is found. The subroutine is a mild example of the search problem that is so frequently encountered in AI. Since the number of paths from the initial square to the goal square is quite small when the board contains only nine squares, the problem is by no means acute in KINGMOVE. But if the board were enlarged only slightly, to, say, 5 × 5, the problem would start to become a significant one.

In this or any other AI program, *heuristics* can be employed to shorten the amount of search that would otherwise be necessary. A heuristic is a simple rule of thumb which serves to reduce the number of alternative possible solutions that must be explored.

A heuristic device is built into line 310 of this subroutine. The king's moves that are generated in this line are always *forward;* that is, the king is never allowed to move backwards, which would be a waste of time. Other heuristics could easily be devised. For instance, the program might be altered so that if it tried a certain path, say,

12369

which turned out to be incorrect, the incorrect path could never be generated again. If this change were made, the program would no longer try the same incorrect path several times in the course of looking for the solution.

On the subject of range it is easy to see that the present version of KINGMOVE is able to solve only a very narrow set of problems (as a matter of fact, it can solve just *one* problem). The range of the program could, with some effort, be extended: It could be made to solve shortest-path problems on a board of arbitrary size; the piece that is moved from square to square could be any chess piece, such as a knight or a rook, rather than being limited to the king; instead of shortest-path problems we might want to make the program find all paths from the initial square to the goal square that require, say, four moves; etc.

But if we continued to extend the range of the program, its efficiency would doubtless begin to suffer. It would take longer for individual problems to be solved, and the amount of memory needed for the program would inevitably begin to increase at an exponential rate.

KINGMOVE Listing

Here is the complete program:

```
1 '              KINGMOVE
2 CLEAR 600

10 '             Supervisor
20 GOSUB 90      ' Initialization
30 GOSUB 150     ' Set array to initial piece arrangement
40 GOSUB 190     ' Draw board
50 GOSUB 410     ' Print current king position
60 GOSUB 290     ' King's move
70 GOSUB 410
80 GOTO 60
```

```
90 '           Initialization
100 CLS
110 RANDOM
120 CU = 1
130 K$ = CHR$(174) + CHR$(157) + STRING$(5, 32) + CHR$(26) +
    STRING$(12, 24) + STRING$(3, 32) + CHR$(188) +
    STRING$(4, 131) + CHR$(188) + CHR$(26) + STRING$(6, 24) +
    CHR$(191) + STRING$(4, 176) + CHR$(191)
140 E$ = STRING$(4, 8) + STRING$(10, 32) + CHR$(26) +
    STRING$(10, 8) + CHR$(26) + STRING$(10, 32)
145 RETURN

150 '           Set array to initial piece arrangement
160 A$(1) = K$: A$(2) = E$: A$(3) = E$: A$(4) = E$: A$(5) = E$
170 A$(6) = E$: A$(7) = E$: A$(8) = E$: A$(9) = E$
180 RETURN

190 '           Draw board
200 V$ = CHR$(195) + CHR$(191) + CHR$(208) + CHR$(191) +
    CHR$(209) + CHR$(191) + CHR$(208) + CHR$(191) + CHR$(200)
210 PRINT: PRINT V$ V$ V$ V$ V$ V$ V$ V$ V$ V$ V$ V$ V$ V$;
220 PRINT @ 3, STRING$(53, 176);
230 PRINT @ 324, STRING$(51, 140);
240 PRINT @ 644, STRING$(51, 140);
250 PRINT @ 963, STRING$(53, 131);
260 POKE 15700, 191: POKE 15718, 191
270 POKE 16020, 191: POKE 16038, 191
280 RETURN

290 '           King's move
300 ST$ = "1"
310 R2 = RND(4): IF R2 = 2 THEN 310
320 IF R2 = 1 THEN IF CU = 3 OR CU = 6 THEN 310
330 IF R2 = 4 THEN IF CU = 3 OR CU = 7 THEN 310
340 IF CU + R2 > 9 THEN 310
350 OC = CU: CU = CU + R2
360 ST$ = ST$ + MID$(STR$(CU), 2, 1)
370 GOSUB 410
380 IF CU = 9 THEN OC = CU: CU = 1: ELSE 310
390 IF LEN(ST$) = 3 THEN PRINT @ 442, "SHORT-";: PRINT @ 506,
    "EST";: PRINT @ 570, "PATH:";: PRINT @ 634, ST$;: GOTO 390
400 RETURN

410 '           Print current king position
420 A$(OC) = E$: A$(CU) = K$
430 FOR I = 1 TO 75: NEXT I
440 PRINT @ 138, A$(1);: PRINT @ 156, A$(2);
450 PRINT @ 173, A$(3);: PRINT @ 457, A$(4);
460 PRINT @ 475, A$(5);: PRINT @ 492, A$(6);
470 PRINT @ 777, A$(7);: PRINT @ 795, A$(8);
480 PRINT @ 813, A$(9);
490 RETURN
```

CHAPTER 2

Game-Playing Programs

"No computer can play even an amateur-level game of chess." Shortly after he made this remark in the mid-1960s, philosopher Hubert Dreyfus of Berkeley was beaten by a computer running MACHAC, a chess program. Dreyfus was surprised by his defeat because he had a deeply felt belief that skill in chess necessitates various uniquely human traits (for example, creativity, intuition, etc.). What this view fails to take into account is that a "uniquely human" trait, such as creativity, when analyzed down to its most basic constituents, may be nothing more than a simple physiological sequence of events which can be imitated (and perhaps even improved upon) by a computer program.

But, as a matter of fact, few of the game-playing programs which have been developed try to play the game in question, whether it's chess, checkers, or Go, by imitating the thought processes that take place in the human mind when occupied in playing the same game. Most of them incorporate evaluation functions which, although they resemble human thought processes to some degree, are not deliberate models of the human mind.

An exception is the checkers program of Arthur L. Samuel. Samuel, formerly IBM's Director of Research, built a learning device into his program so that its play improved over a period as it learned from experience. Samuel's program today plays a formidable game of checkers, though it is not quite of master caliber.

A program that *is* a master-level checkers player, according to its creators, is the Duke University checkers program. This program is reputedly very strong on the number of moves it can look ahead. The program's authors, Eric C. Jensen and Tom R. Truscott, believe it to be about the tenth strongest checkers player in the world. Not surprisingly, this is disputed by master players.

The game-playing program that has performed best to date against a strong human player is Hans Berliner's BKG 9.8, which plays the ancient game of backgammon. In a match against the backgammon world champion, Luigi Villa, BKG won decisively, taking four games out of the five-game match. The program was run on a PDP-10 at Carnegie-Mellon University in Pittsburg; the moves were relayed to the match site at Monte Carlo by satellite.

The Evaluation Function

What goes into the writing of a chess or checkers program? The first step is to develop an *exact* and *precise* method to determine, when it is the computer's turn to play, which move is best under the circumstances that prevail. This is called an *evaluation function*. An evaluation function for chess or any other game must be specific enough so that it can be translated into a computer program. Some nebulous theory of, for instance, strategic or positional factors would be impossible to embody in a computer chess program without further refinement of the theory into more precise terms.

Two programming methods which are commonly found as part of the evaluation functions of game-playing programs are *minimaxing* and the *alpha-beta algorithm*. Let's consider them briefly.

Trees and Minimaxing

Let's assume that a human is playing a game of chess with a computer. The human has just moved. It's the computer's turn to play. What does the program do?

A logical way to proceed, one which many programmers have chosen, is to build a *tree* of possible moves. The program looks ahead, say, six moves (three white moves and three black). Within this six-move limitation the computer figures *every* combination of moves that can possibly be made by either side. Furthermore, for each possible move, the computer assigns a numeric value to the resulting position of the board; this numeric value indicates whether the computer or its opponent is ahead in that particular board position and is based on factors such as material and position.

When the computer has generated the entire tree it traces back along the branches of the tree, looking for the sequence of moves that will bring it the greatest advantage, *always assuming that its opponent will make the best possible moves available*. This technique is called *minimaxing,* since the computer makes moves that bring it maximum gain, and makes the natural assumption that its opponent will make moves that bring the computer minimum gain. When the computer has determined just what this sequence of moves is, it chooses the first move in the sequence as its move.

Alpha-Beta Algorithm

Given tree and minimaxing procedures, it might seem the best way for a chess program to proceed would be to generate all possible moves down to a deph of, say, fifty moves, instead of being limited to six moves as in the preceding example. If a computer could do this, it would of course play a perfect game; the computer would in effect have a forced win from the first move!

The problem with creating a tree this deep is the enormous number of positions the computer would be forced to evaluate. I.J. Good estimated that with a fifty-move limit, there are $10^{15,790}$ possible games of chess. This is a number so huge that the word "astronomic" cannot begin to describe it, since there is no phenomenon in the realm of astronomy which requires a number this large to describe it. Obviously, the number of positions that are available for evaluation must somehow be reduced. One way to do this is by limiting the depth of the search; the program's "lookahead" can be set to four ply (that is, four moves ahead, in the terminology invented by Samuel), or seven ply, eleven ply, or some other convenient figure, depending on such factors as the speed of the program and the patience of the computer's human opponent.

Another way to limit the amount of searching is by means of the alpha-beta algorithm. The idea behind the alpha-beta algorithm is simple. When the computer is generating the tree of possible moves, it need not bother to generate a branch of the tree which is the result of an inferior move on the part of the computer. In other words, once the computer evaluates move X and realizes that it's a bad one, it is no longer necessary to generate the subsidiary moves leading from move X and evaluate them, since the computer isn't going to make move X anyway. Similarly —once again following the minimax approach—the computer does not need to generate a branch of the tree which is the result of an inferior move on the part of the computer's opponent.

When the alpha-beta algorithm is employed as part of a tree search, the savings in time that is realized is phenomenal. David Levy estimates that under optimal conditions, a four-ply search incorporating the alpha-beta algorithm can be conducted 500 times faster than a non-alpha-beta search.

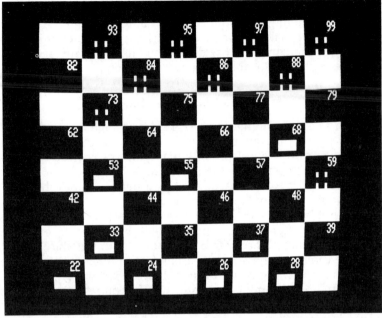

Fig. 2-1. Video display of computer running CHECKERS.

CHECKERS

Below is a listing of CHECKERS, a checkers-playing program. Fig. 2-1 shows a video display of a computer running this program. In the interest of brevity CHECKERS does not incorporate a move-by-move tree generation procedure as previously described. The program looks ahead from one to two moves, depending on the situation.

Before we discuss the complete listing, let's take a look at some of the major subroutines.

Supervisor

First let's examine the supervisor routine:

```
10  '               Supervisor
20  GOSUB 130       ' Initialization
30  GOSUB 230       ' Set array to initial piece configuration
40  GOSUB 970       ' Computer's first move
50  GOSUB 450       ' Draw checkerboard
60  GOSUB 570       ' Print nos. on squares & crnt arngmt pieces
70  GOSUB 780       ' Input
80  GOSUB 840       ' Change array to reflect new posn of pieces
90  GOSUB 570
100 IF M$ = "X" THEN GOTO 70       ' Double and triple jumps
110 GOSUB 1040      ' Evaluation routine
120 GOTO 60
```

This routine calls the subroutines of the program as they are needed. The initialization subroutine is called first. This subroutine takes care of a few housekeeping tasks, such as clearing the display, reseeding the random-number generator, setting up an array, and assigning values to some global variables.

Next, the subroutine that sets the array to the initial piece configuration is called. In CHECKERS the checkerboard and its arrangement of pieces are represented as (a) a graphics routine on the display, which is convenient for the player but inconvenient for the computer, and as (b) an array, which is handy for the computer although not directly visible to the player. Why does an 11 × 11 array need to be dimensioned when a checkerboard contains only 64 squares? Because, as a result of the evaluation function we have chosen, the program needs an array that is larger than the minimum. If we tried to use an 8 × 8 (64-unit) array, sooner or later the program would try to assign a value to a negative array element. For example,

$$T\$(I - 2, J) = WH\$$$

where $1 = 1$. Since BASIC makes no provision for negative arrays, an error of some sort would result.

The subroutine that chooses the computer's first move is next. The computer always has the black pieces. Since Black always moves first in checkers, the computer always has the first move, which simplifies the programming a bit. The subroutine simply picks one of four opening moves at random.

The next subroutine to be called draws the checkerboard on the screen. Since this is a graphics routine, just how it is done is very much dependent on your particular computer and its BASIC.

The subroutine beginning at line 570 is also rather dependent on your brand of BASIC. This subroutine prints numbers on the checkerboard squares, so the player can let the program know what move he or she wants to make by specifying the numbers of the squares involved. These numbers correspond to the array elements. For instance, the square numbered 55 on the screen corresponds to the array element T$(5, 5). This subroutine also prints the current arrangement of pieces on the board. Your BASIC may require separate items in a print list (such as the print lists contained in lines 620 and 710) to be separated by semicolons.

The input subroutine allows the player to enter a move. Since INKEY$ is used, a carriage return at the end of the input is not required; the program needs only five keystrokes. These five keystrokes are (a) the two digits of the number of the square the player is moving from, (b) a "-" (hyphen), unless the player is making a double or triple jump or is setting up a board position, in which case "X" should be typed, and (c) the two digits of the number of the square the player is moving to.

Next comes the subroutine at 840, which changes the array to reflect the new piece positions which result after the player inputs his move.

If the player has typed "X" as part of the input, line 100 sends program control back to the input subroutine, and it's the player's turn to move once again. This allows White to make double and triple jumps.

Evaluation Routine

The final subroutine is the longest and by far the most important. This is the evaluation routine, in which the computer (Black) decides which move to make. The evaluation routine is based on the following algorithm:

1. If Black is in a position to capture one of White's men, Black does so. If not, then
2. If one of Black's men is being threatened with capture by one of White's men, Black guards against the capture if possible. If it's not possible, or if no capture is imminent, then
3. Black makes the first available move which won't result in a capture of the man being moved.

As you can see, this is a simple, uncomplicated algorithm which mainly serves to keep Black out of trouble. This results in a checkers program which is not particularly aggressive, though it usually manages to defend itself adequately.

Here is the evaluation routine:

```
1040 '              Evaluation routine
1050 '              A. Black looking for jump possibilities
1060 FOR I = 2 TO 9
1070 FOR J = 2 TO 9
1080 IF T$(I, J) = BL$ THEN 1090 ELSE 1110
1090 IF T$(I - 1, J + 1) = WH$ AND T$(I - 2, J + 2) = X$ THEN
     T$(I - 1, J + 1) = X$: T$(I - 2, J + 2) = BL$:
     T$(I, J) = X$: GOTO 1360
1100 IF T$(I - 1, J - 1) = WH$ AND T$(I - 2, J - 2) = X$ THEN
     T$(I - 1, J - 1) = X$: T$(I - 2, J - 2) = BL$: T$(I, J) =
     X$: GOTO 1360
1110 NEXT J, I
1120 '              B. Black guarding itself against a jump
1130 FOR I = 2 TO 9
1140 FOR J = 2 TO 9
1150 IF T$(I, J) = BL$ THEN 1160 ELSE 1220
1160 IF T$(I - 1, J - 1) = WH$ AND T$(I + 1, J + 1) = X$
     THEN 1180
1170 IF T$(I - 1, J + 1) = WH$ AND T$(I + 1, J - 1) = X$
     THEN 1200 ELSE 1220
1180 IF T$(I + 2, J) = BL$ THEN T$(I + 2, J) = X$:
     T$(I + 1, J + 1) = BL$: GOTO 1360
1190 IF T$(I + 2, J + 2) = BL$ THEN T$(I + 2, J + 2) = X$:
     T$(I + 1, J + 1) = BL$: GOTO 1360
1200 IF T$(I + 2, J - 2) = BL$ THEN T$(I + 2, J - 2) = X$:
     T$(I + 1, J - 1) = BL$: GOTO 1360
1210 IF T$(I + 2, J) = BL$ THEN T$(I + 2, J) = X$:
     T$(I + 1, J - 1) = BL$: GOTO 1360
1220 NEXT J, I
1230 '              C. Black looking for a move which won't result
1240 '                 in a capture
1250 FOR I = 2 TO 9
1260 FOR J = 2 TO 9
1270 IF T$(I, J) = BL$ THEN 1280 ELSE 1340
1280 IF T$(I - 2, J) = WH$ AND T$(I, J - 2) = X$ THEN 1310
1290 IF T$(I - 2, J - 2) = WH$ THEN 1310
1300 IF T$(I - 1, J - 1) = X$ THEN T$(I, J) = X$:
     T$(I - 1, J - 1) = BL$: GOTO 1360
1310 IF T$(I - 2, J) = WH$ AND T$(I, J + 2) = X$ THEN 1340
1320 IF T$(I - 2, J + 2) = WH$ THEN 1340
1330 IF T$(I - 1, J + 1) = X$ THEN T$(I, J) = X$:
     T$(I - 1, J + 1) = BL$: GOTO 1360
1340 NEXT J, I
1350 '              Reset edges of array to the empty string
1360 FOR I = 0 TO 1: FOR J = 0 TO 1: T$(I, J) = "": NEXT J, I
1370 FOR I = 10 TO 11: FOR J = 10 TO 11: T$(I, J) ="":NEXT J,I
1380 RETURN
```

The routine is divided into three major parts. Part A, in which
Black looks for jump possibilities, corresponds to part 1 of the
algorithm above. Part B, in which Black guards against a jump,
corresponds to part 2 of the algorithm, and part C, in which Black
looks for a move which won't result in a capture (of Black's own
man) corresponds to part 3. The organization is hierarchical. If
Black finds no move to be made under part A of the subroutine,
control falls through to part B. If no move is found there, control
falls through again to part C.

Let's dissect part A of the subroutine and find exactly how it works. Part A is set within a double FOR. . .NEXT loop; each of the two FOR. . .NEXT variables cycles from 2 to 9, ensuring that the entire board is taken into consideration.

Line 1080 sifts through every square on the board, looking for a Black piece. When one is found, lines 1090 and 1100 take over. They look for a special situation which can occur on any two of four adjacent squares: the situation where a White piece can be captured.

Let's assume that a Black piece has been located at T$(6, 6) in the array (which corresponds to square 66 on the board). This situation is illustrated in Fig. 2-2. Line 1090 looks for a White piece at T$(I − 1, J + 1), which is square 57, and an empty square at

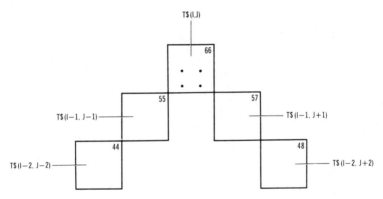

Fig. 2-2. Capture squares.

T$(I − 2, J + 2) (square 48). If both of these conditions are satisfied, an empty square is placed in the array at T$(I − 1, J + 1) (square 57) and T$ (I, J) (square 66), and a Black piece is placed at T$(I − 2, J + 2) (square 48). Black has captured White's man. Control now passes out of the evaluation routine entirely (after a brief re-initialization at lines 1360 and 1370). If, on the other hand, one or both of the conditions are not met, control passes to line 1100, which looks for a jump situation on squares 55 and 44. Only four squares need to be considered when the program is looking for a jump; the squares in back of Black's man can be ignored since only kings can move backwards, and CHECKERS does not allow Black kings. (A White piece, however, is automatically kinged when it reaches Black's first rank.) If no jump situation exists at any of the four squares, control passes to sections B and C of the subroutine, which make their evaluations in much the same fashion as section A.

The evaluation routine that we've chosen for CHECKERS is not elegant, but it is workable, mainly because the range of moves that a checkers piece can make is quite limited.

CHECKERS Listing

Here is the complete program:

```
1 '             CHECKERS, Vers. 1.1
2 CLEAR 1500

10 '            Supervisor
20 GOSUB 130        ' Initialization
30 GOSUB 230        ' Set array to initial piece configuration
40 GOSUB 970        ' Computer's first move
50 GOSUB 450        ' Draw checkerboard
60 GOSUB 570        ' Print nos. on squares & crnt arngmt pieces
70 GOSUB 780        ' Input
80 GOSUB 840        ' Change array to reflect new posn of pieces
90 GOSUB 570
100 IF M$ = "X" THEN GOTO 70      ' Double and triple jumps
110 GOSUB 1040      ' Evaluation routine
120 GOTO 60

130 '           Initialization
140 CLS
150 RANDOM
160 DIM T$(11, 11)
170 BL$ = CHR$(162) + " " + CHR$(162)
180 WH$ = STRING$(4, 143)
200 KWH$ = CHR$(143) + CHR$(75) + CHR$(143) + CHR$(143)
210 X$ = STRING$(5, " ")
220 RETURN

230 '           Set array to initial piece configuration
240 FOR I = 2 TO 9
250 FOR J = 2 TO 9
260 T$(I, J) = X$
270 NEXT J, I
280 FOR I = 2 TO 4 STEP 2
290 FOR J = 2 TO 8 STEP 2
300 T$(I, J) = WH$
310 NEXT J, I
320 FOR I = 3 TO 3
330 FOR J = 3 TO 9 STEP 2
340 T$(I, J) = WH$
350 NEXT J, I
360 FOR I = 7 TO 9 STEP 2
370 FOR J = 3 TO 9 STEP 2
380 T$(I, J) = BL$
390 NEXT J, I
400 FOR I = 8 TO 8
410 FOR J = 2 TO 8 STEP 2
420 T$(I, J) = BL$
430 NEXT J, I
440 RETURN
```

```
450 '           Draw checkerboard
460 DEFSTR A-D
470 B = STRING$(8, 191)
480 C = STRING$(8, " ")
490 A = B + C + B + C + B + C + B + C
500 D = C + B + C + B + C + B + C + B
510 PRINT A;A;D;D;A;A;D;D;A;A;D;D;A;A;D;C;B;C;B;C;B;C;
520 FOR I = 16376 TO 16383
530 POKE I, 191
540 NEXT I
550 DEFSNG A-D
560 RETURN

570 '           Print numbers on checkerboard squares and
580 '           print current arrangement of pieces
590 L = 13
600 FOR I = 9 TO 3 STEP -2
610 FOR J = 3 TO 9 STEP 2
620 PRINT @ L, RIGHT$(STR$(I), 1) RIGHT$(STR$(J), 1);
630 PRINT @ L + 61, T$(I, J);
640 L = L + 16
650 NEXT J
660 L = L + 192
670 NEXT I
680 L = 133
690 FOR I = 8 TO 2 STEP -2
700 FOR J = 2 TO 8 STEP 2
710 PRINT @ L, RIGHT$(STR$(I), 1) RIGHT$(STR$(J), 1);
720 PRINT @ L + 61, T$(I, J);
730 L = L + 16
740 NEXT J
750 L = L + 192
760 NEXT I
770 RETURN

780 '           Input
790 B$ = ""
800 A$ = INKEY$: IF A$ = "" THEN 800
810 B$ = B$ + A$
820 IF LEN(B$) = 5 THEN 830 ELSE 800
830 RETURN

840 '           Change the array to reflect new board position
850 I = VAL(LEFT$(B$, 1)): J = VAL(MID$(B$, 2, 1))
860 K = VAL(MID$(B$, 4, 1)): L = VAL(RIGHT$(B$, 1))
870 M$ = MID$(B$, 3, 1)
880 IF K = I - 2 AND L = J - 2 THEN T$(K, L) = KWH$:
    T$(I, J) = X$: T$(I - 1, J - 1) = X$: GOTO 960
890 IF K = I - 2 AND L = J + 2 THEN T$(K, L) = KWH$:
    T$(I, J) = X$: T$(I - 1, J + 1) = X$: GOTO 960
900 IF K = 9 THEN T$(K, L) = KWH$: GOTO 930
910 IF T$(I, J) = KWH$ THEN T$(K, L) = KWH$: GOTO 930
920 T$(K, L) = WH$
930 T$(I, J) = X$
940 IF K = I + 2 AND L = J + 2 THEN T$(K - 1, L - 1) = X$:
    GOTO 960
950 IF K = I + 2 AND L = J - 2 THEN T$(K - 1, L + 1) = X$
960 RETURN
```

```
970 '              Computer's first move
980 RAN = RND(4)
990 IF RAN = 1 THEN T$(7, 3) = X$: T$(6, 4) = BL$
1000 IF RAN = 2 THEN T$(7, 5) = X$: T$(6, 4) = BL$
1010 IF RAN = 3 THEN T$(7, 5) = X$: T$(6, 6) = BL$
1020 IF RAN = 4 THEN T$(7, 7) = X$: T$(6, 6) = BL$
1030 RETURN

1040 '              Evaluation routine
1050 '              A. Black looking for Jump possibilities
1060 FOR I = 2 TO 9
1070 FOR J = 2 TO 9
1080 IF T$(I, J) = BL$ THEN 1090 ELSE 1110
1090 IF T$(I - 1, J + 1) = WH$ AND T$(I - 2, J + 2) = X$ THEN
     T$(I - 1, J + 1) = X$: T$(I - 2, J + 2) = BL$:
     T$(I, J) = X$: GOTO 1360
1100 IF T$(I - 1, J - 1) = WH$ AND T$(I - 2, J - 2) = X$ THEN
     T$(I - 1, J - 1) = X$: T$(I - 2, J - 2) = BL$: T$(I, J) =
     X$: GOTO 1360
1110 NEXT J, I
1120 '              B. Black guarding itself against a jump
1130 FOR I = 2 TO 9
1140 FOR J = 2 TO 9
1150 IF T$(I, J) = BL$ THEN 1160 ELSE 1220
1160 IF T$(I - 1, J - 1) = WH$ AND T$(I + 1, J + 1) = X$
     THEN 1180
1170 IF T$(I - 1, J + 1) = WH$ AND T$(I + 1, J - 1) = X$
     THEN 1200 ELSE 1220
1180 IF T$(I + 2, J) = BL$ THEN T$(I + 2, J) = X$:
     T$(I + 1, J + 1) = BL$: GOTO 1360
1190 IF T$(I + 2, J + 2) = BL$ THEN T$(I + 2, J + 2) = X$:
     T$(I + 1, J + 1) = BL$: GOTO 1360
1200 IF T$(I + 2, J - 2) = BL$ THEN T$(I + 2, J - 2) = X$:
     T$(I + 1, J - 1) = BL$: GOTO 1360
1210 IF T$(I + 2, J) = BL$ THEN T$(I + 2, J) = X$:
     T$(I + 1, J - 1) = BL$: GOTO 1360
1220 NEXT J, I
1230 '              C. Black looking for a move which won't result
1240 '                 in a capture
1250 FOR I = 2 TO 9
1260 FOR J = 2 TO 9
1270 IF T$(I, J) = BL$ THEN 1280 ELSE 1340
1280 IF T$(I - 2, J) = WH$ AND T$(I, J - 2) = X$ THEN 1310
1290 IF T$(I - 2, J - 2) = WH$ THEN 1310
1300 IF T$(I - 1, J - 1) = X$ THEN T$(I, J) = X$:
     T$(I - 1, J - 1) = BL$: GOTO 1360
1310 IF T$(I - 2, J) = WH$ AND T$(I, J + 2) = X$ THEN 1340
1320 IF T$(I - 2, J + 2) = WH$ THEN 1340
1330 IF T$(I - 1, J + 1) = X$ THEN T$(I, J) = X$:
     T$(I - 1, J + 1) = BL$: GOTO 1360
1340 NEXT J, I
1350 '              Reset edges of array to the empty string
1360 FOR I = 0 TO 1: FOR J = 0 TO 1: T$(I, J) = "": NEXT J, I
1370 FOR I = 10 TO 11: FOR J = 10 TO 11: T$(I, J) ="":NEXT J,I
1380 RETURN
```

Possible Modifications

If you found this program interesting, you might want to change it or improve upon it. If so, here are some suggestions:

(1) Write a routine to allow Black kings and double and triple jumps (the program as written reserves these privileges for White alone).

(2) Change the evaluation routine to allow a greater lookahead (three ply or deeper).

(3) Incorporate various checkers theories, such as the importance of control of the center, into the evaluation routine so that the program will choose its moves in accordance with these theories.

(4) Change the program so that the computer will alternately take Black and White, i.e., play against itself.

CHAPTER 3

Problem Solving

Computers have been used for solving problems of business, science, and industry almost since the first one rolled off the assembly line. But the problem-solving ability of computers to date, while impressive, is not as deep or wide ranging as it could be. Programs can be written which solve complicated problems in such fields as mathematical analysis, statistics, navigation, celestial mechanics, and so on, but the area in which any one particular program can operate must be very narrowly defined by the programmer. Furthermore, as might be expected, the harder it is for a human to solve some specific problem, such as proving a complex theorem of mathematics, the harder it is to write a program to do something similar.

Many researchers, therefore, are interested in making computers solve a wider range of more challenging problems than before. In this chapter we will examine two of the programs they have developed: Thomas G. Evans's geometric analogy program and Newell, Shaw, and Simon's General Problem Solver (GPS). Then we will look at a problem-solving program written in familiar, homely BASIC. This program is called TF, and the problem it attempts to solve is an interesting one: the prediction of human behavior.

The Geometric Analogy Program

Most IQ tests are divided into three parts. One part tests mathematical abilities; one part tests verbal abilities; the remaining part tests the ability to visualize and find analogies among geometric figures.

A geometric analogy program, written by Thomas G. Evans in 1963, solves the sort of geometric-analogy problems commonly found in IQ tests, and does a very good job of it, too. The program operates in a beautifully simple, straightforward way; it reduces the task of solving geometric-analogy problems to a mechanical process. A problem of this type is shown in Fig. 3-1. Let's see how the Evans program would attempt to solve it.

There are seven figures in Fig. 3-1; they are labelled 1, 2, 3, a, b, c, and d. The problem the program is required to solve can be stated thus: 1 is to 2 as 3 is to a, b, c, or d?

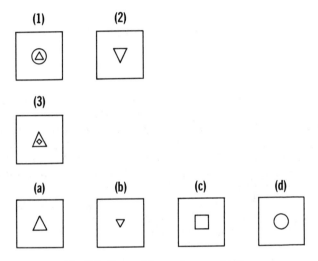

Fig. 3-1. Geometric analogy problem.

If we stop to consider, we will see that the solution to this problem revolves around the *comparison of transformations*. To understand what is meant by this, notice that five pairs of figures are involved. These pairs of figures are:

$$1:2$$
$$3:a$$
$$3:b$$
$$3:c$$
$$3:d$$

Each pair of figures represents a transformation. For instance, the pair 1:2 represents a figure, 1, which has in some way been transformed into the figure 2. The job of the program is to determine what this transformation between 1 and 2 is, and decide which of the pairs 3:a, 3:b, 3:c, or 3:d represents the same transformation (or most nearly the same).

The first thing the program must do is build a representation of the important positional features of each of the geometric figures. If we let p stand for a circle, q for an equilateral triangle, and r for a square, the representation that is built up for each of the figures in Fig. 3-1 would look something like this:

$1 = q$ inside p
$2 = q$
$3 = r$ inside q
$a = q$
$b = q$
$c = r$
$d = p$

Notice that the only positional relationship in the list above is *inside*. Other relationships that could develop, depending on the figure, are *above, to the left of,* etc.

After the program has generated the representations, it checks each pair of figures to see how the figure on the right-hand side of the transformation has been altered from the figure on the left-hand side. The result would be:

1:2 p deleted
q scale change $\times$ 2
q rotated 60 degrees

3:a r deleted

3:b q scale change $\times$ $\frac{1}{2}$
q rotated 60 degrees
r deleted

3:c q deleted
r scale change $\times$ 2
r rotated 45 degrees

3:d q deleted
r deleted

The final step is to compare the transformations for pairs 3:a, 3:b, 3:c, and 3:d with the transformation for the 1:2 pair. Whichever of the 3:a, 3:b, 3:c, 3:d transformations most nearly matches the 1:2 transformation is the answer. In this particular instance, the program would choose c as its answer.

Notice that a human attempting to solve this problem might well use many of the same methods that were employed by the program. The human problem-solver would probably look at the

1:2 pair, determine how 1 had been transformed to produce 2, and then try to find an analogous pair from among the 3:a, 3:b, 3:c, and 3:d pairs that involved the same transformation. This is exactly what Evans's program does.

This implies that Evans used his own thought processes as a model in the course of writing the program. While this technique succeeds admirably here, imitating human thought processes isn't always the best way to perform some "intelligent" procedure, and, in fact, may be a grossly inefficient way of doing things, rather like counting on one's fingers instead of using a calculator. Perhaps it would even be possible to improve the Evans program if an algorithm which wasn't based on human thought processes were used to select the best figure-pair. But the problem in doing so is evident; it would be more difficult to find and incorporate into a program a fresh, completely new way of performing some task rather than making use of an algorithm which is seemingly built into our brains.

The General Problem Solver

If the geometric analogy program makes implicit use of human thought processes as part of its problem-solving strategy, the General Problem Solver (GPS) does so quite explicitly and was in fact written to embody certain psychological theories of human problem-solving.

The geometric analogy program can operate on one class of problems and one class only. GPS, as its name implies, can solve a much wider range of problems, though this range is by no means limitless.

GPS utilizes two vital categories of data called *states* and *operators*. To understand what is meant by states and operators, let's look at an example.

Suppose you get in your car and turn the starter. The car doesn't start. You make several attempts to crank it up, but it refuses to start. You have a problem.

The problem can be defined in terms of states. "State" as we are using the term may be considered an abbreviation for "state of affairs." The problem has an *initial state* and a *goal state*. The initial state simply refers to the beginning situation of the problem, i.e., the car won't start. The goal state is the situation which you desire to reach: the car's engine turning properly. This is depicted graphically in Fig. 3-2.

Inspecting Fig. 3-2, we can see that the goal state contains something which is not in the initial state. This thing which the goal state contains is called the *difference* between the two states.

INITIAL
STATE

CAR
INOPERATIVE

Fig. 3-2. Problem expressed in terms
of states.

CAR
OPERATIVE

GOAL
STATE

The difference between the initial state of *car inoperative* and the goal state of *car operative* could be expressed as, simply, *engine turning*. Notice that to get from the initial state of the goal state, the difference between the two states must be reduced to zero.

Now, back to the car. You get out, open the hood, and peer down at the engine. You detect a strong odor of gasoline, and you realize that the engine is flooded. To get the car started you will need to press the accelerator all the way to the floor and hold it there as you turn the starter. (This sweeps excess gasoline out of the carburetor by causing the choke and throttle valves to open wide.)

You have just developed an *operator*. An operator is a rule which, when applied to state *X*, will cause state *X* to be transformed into state *Y*. An operator is represented graphically by an arrow (Fig. 3-3).

Your object is to reduce the *difference* between the initial state and the goal state to zero. The initial state is *car inoperative*, the goal state is *car operative*, and the difference between the initial

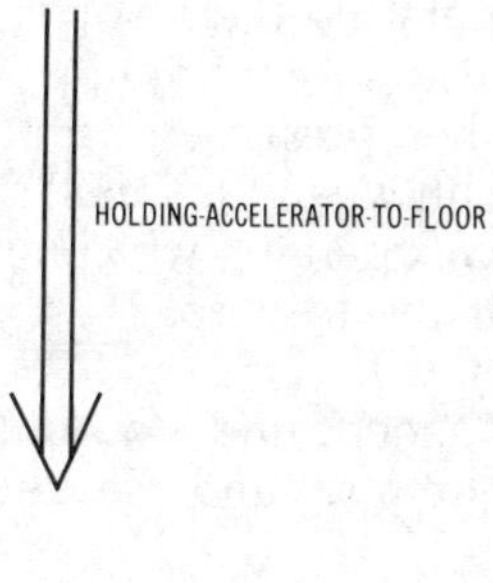

Fig. 3-3. Operator.

HOLDING-ACCELERATOR-TO-FLOOR

state and the goal state is *engine turning.* So all you have to do, apparently, to reduce the difference between the two states to zero (thereby transforming the initial state into the goal state) is apply the holding-accelerator-to-floor operator to the initial state.

However, the holding-accelerator-to-floor operator cannot be applied to the initial state. Why? Because you still remain outside of your car (eyeing the engine, no doubt, with something less than love). You must be inside, in the driver's seat, in order to be able to utilize the holding-accelerator-to-floor operator! So you establish an *intermediate goal,* which we'll call *driver seated in car,* which can be reached from the initial state by means of the operator get-into-car.

Now all the pieces of the puzzle have been assembled and the problem of getting your car started is ready to be solved:

1. Find the difference between the initial state and the intermediate state, which is *seated in car.*
2. Reduce the difference between the initial state and the intermediate state to zero by applying the proper operator, which is get-into-car, to the initial state. At this point you have arrived at the intermediate state.
3. Find the difference between the intermediate state and the goal state, which is *engine running.*
4. Reduce the difference to zero by applying the proper operator, which is press-accelerator-to-floor.

You have come to the goal state; the problem is solved. The entire process is summed up in Fig. 3-4.

The preceding account is not meant to imply, of course, that a person is ever consciously aware of going through all of these steps while trying to solve the problem of getting a flooded engine started or any other type of problem. But, according to at least one theory of human problem-solving, this is a fair representation of the internal processes that could take place in a person who was engaged in solving a problem, even though he or she would not be aware of these processes without a great deal of reflection.

The General Problem Solver finds solutions to problems much the same way as we found a solution to the problem of starting the car. When presented with a task to be solved, it first finds the difference between the initial state and the goal state. Then it tries to apply an operator which will reduce the difference between the two states to zero. If in its repertoire no operator can be found that will do this, GPS establishes as many intermediate states as needed, finds the difference between one intermediate state and the next, and uses the appropriate operator—if available

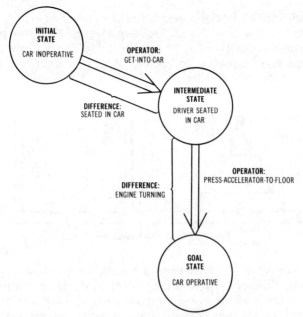

Fig. 3-4. Solution to problem of starting car.

—to reduce the difference between states until the goal state can be reached.

It is important to note that GPS *cannot* devise operators by itself *ex nihilo*. Operators (as well as a host of other material, including a concise statement of the problem itself) must be carefully coded into GPS by a programmer. But it is only fair to point out that humans have the same limitation; in one way or another we must be given most or all of the operators which we use in the process of problem-solving. Someone trying to start a flooded engine wouldn't know that press-accelerator-to-floor was a valid operator unless he or she had obtained this information from a mechanic or other source. The operator might perhaps be deduced from a general knowledge of automobile engines, but the deduction would in turn be based on data which must have come from outside.

What GPS Can Do

GPS can solve a wide variety of tasks. GPS is one unified program—not a collection of smaller programs to perform specialized tasks—yet it can do simple calculus problems, prove theorems of logic, and parse (analyze the syntactic structure of) English sentences. Given any sequence of letters that exhibits a pattern of some sort, it can find the next letters in that sequence. It is able to solve the Tower of Hanoi Problem (Fig. 3-5). In this problem the "tower" on peg 1 must be transferred to peg 3. Only one ring at a time can be placed on another peg. No larger ring may be placed on top of a smaller.

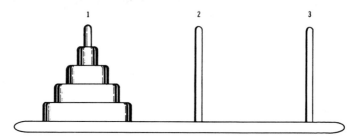

Fig. 3-5. Tower of Hanoi Problem.

It can also find the answer to the well-known Missionaries and Cannibals Problem. There are three missionaries and three cannibals on the bank of a river. The missionaries have a boat, which will carry one or two people. If at any time the missionaries on either side of the two banks are outnumbered by cannibals, those missionaries will be eaten. How can the missionaries get all six people to the opposite bank of the river intact? GPS took 16 minutes to solve this problem; the reader might care to try solving it and compare his or her time with that of GPS.

TF

Now we are going to consider a problem-solving program, TF, which is written in BASIC. TF is a sort of predictive game. It tries to predict what action the player is next going to take, based on its observation of the player's past behavior. The player types at random the letter T or the letter F; the program's job is to figure out which letter the player is going to type next.

Ordinarily, of course, there is no way of telling what an element of a random sequence will be just by examining the previous elements; that's why it's a *random* sequence. But the assumption was made, during the course of writing TF, that a person's behavior can never be *truly* random; no matter how much the player tries to randomize his or her responses, there may be certain patterns in the player's actions of which he or she is completely unaware. So the program stores every response, whether T or F, and searches for patterns in the player's behavior. If it finds a pattern, then if the pattern occurs again later, the program will be in a

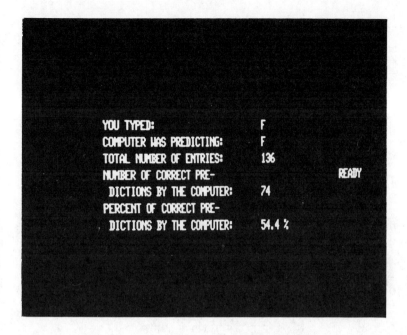

Fig. 3-6. Video display of computer running TF.

position to make a prediction. Fig. 3-6 shows a video display of a computer running the TF program.

Supervisor

Here is the TF supervisor:

```
100 '          Supervisor
110 GOSUB 190    ' Initialization
120 GOSUB 250    ' First LE inputs from player
130 GOSUB 310    ' Input
140 GOSUB 550    ' Printing and scorekeeping
150 GOSUB 380    ' Location update
160 GOSUB 490    ' Match-pattern update
170 GOSUB 420    ' Location calculation
180 GOTO 130
```

The supervisor controls seven subroutines. Two of them are called once, at the beginning of the program. The remaining five subroutines form a loop and are called repeatedly as the program executes.

Initial Routines

The first subroutine that is called is the initialization sequence:

```
190 '          Initialization
200 RANDOM
210 DIM Q(1111, 2)
220 LE = 4
230 CLS
240 RETURN
```

LE (for "length") is set to 4 by line 220. To understand what this variable is for, imagine that someone who is playing TF types in the following sequence:

F F T F T T T F T F

The first letter that was typed is F, the second F, the third T, and so on.

Each time a letter is typed, the program establishes a current *match pattern*. The match pattern is simply the last four letters that were typed. So in the example above, the match pattern is:

F F T F T T │T F T F│

or T F T F.

Now suppose the player types F as the next entry:

F F T F T T │T F T F│F

The program updates the match pattern by shifting the "window" one letter to the right:

F F T F T T │F T F F│

and the new match pattern is F T F F.

This explains the purpose of variable LE: it sets the length of the match pattern to four letters.

The subroutine at 250, first LE inputs from player, is called next:

```
250 '          First LE inputs from player
260 FOR I = 1 TO LE
270 GOSUB 310
280 MP(I) = CD
290 NEXT I
300 RETURN
```

When the player types a letter, the letter is coded (T = 1, F = 0) and the code is placed in variable CD. This subroutine takes the player's first four inputs, codes them, and stores them in MP(1), MP(2), MP(3), and MP(4). The effect of the subroutine is to get the first four inputs from the player without making any predictions. This is an attempt to give TF a clue about the player's behavior before it tries any serious predicting.

38

Representation of Data

Each time the player types a new letter, the match pattern (i.e., the previous four letters that the player has typed) is coded into a number, LO. If the letter typed was T, then Q(LO, 1) is incremented. If the letter was F, then Q(LO, 2) is incremented.

The location calculation subroutine finds the value of LO; the location update subroutine does the incrementing. Here is the location calculation subroutine:

```
420 '          Location calculation
430 A$ = ""
440 FOR I = 1 TO LE
450 A$ = A$ + MID$(STR$(MP(I)), 2)
460 NEXT I
470 LO = VAL(A$)
480 RETURN
```

MP(1), MP(2), MP(3), and MP(4) always contain the current match pattern (in coded form). The location calculation subroutine takes these four values, strings them together, and uses the resulting value as the name of an element in array Q that is associated with the match pattern.

For example, suppose the current match pattern is F T T T. This would be coded as 0 1 1 1. The location calculation subroutine takes each of these four numbers, makes them into strings, and gets the second character in the string (which is the number itself; this gets rid of the leading blank). The four strings are concatenated in line 450 and converted from a string back into a number in line 470. Line 430, incidentally, sets A$ to the empty string, *not* to a single blank (this may be a bit unclear from the listing).

Suppose the player now types F. Since the previous four letters were F T T T, the program assumes that in the future, after typing F T T T, the player will have a tendency to type F again. The code for F T T T is 0 1 1 1, which becomes 0111, or 111. This number is stored in variable LO ("location").

The location update subroutine is short:

```
380 '          Location update
390 IF CD = 1 THEN Q(LO, 1) = Q(LO, 1) + 1: GOTO 410
400 IF CD = 0 THEN Q(LO, 2) = Q(LO, 2) + 1
410 RETURN
```

In this subroutine, if the player types F after a particular match pattern, CD is equal to 0, and array location Q(LO, 2) is incremented. If the player types T, CD is equal to 1, and Q(LO, 1) is incremented.

The storage structure developed here is rather wasteful of memory, since an array of 1112 × 3 = 3336 elements has to be dimensioned (line 210) though only 32 of these elements are ever actually needed or used by the program. This method has the advantage of simplicity; if your computer has limited memory (less than 16K RAM), however, you may need to revise the storage structure to make the program more memory-efficient. If so, the revision should prove to be a minor task.

What the Program Is Doing

We have now uncovered the basic algorithms behind TF. Let's look at a concrete example. We'll assume a specific sequence of letters, say F T T T, has been typed by the player ten times in the course of a game with TF. After typing F T T T, let's say that the next letter the player typed was F 80 percent of the time (eight times) and T 20 percent of the time (two times). The program has this information stored away. The next time the player types the sequence F T T T, the program consults array Q. It finds that Q(111, 1) = 2 and Q(111, 2) = 8. Since in the past the player typed F four times as often as T after the sequence F T T T, the program will predict an F as the player's next letter. If Q(111, 1) = Q(111, 2), or if the player hasn't used the sequence F T T T yet, the program generates a random T or F as its prediction.

The player now types, say, T. Since the program was predicting an F, the program has made an incorrect prediction. This fact is noted and printed on the display, along with a running score of how well the program is doing. The sequence is now F T T T T. The match-pattern update subroutine is called. The match-pattern "window" is "bumped" one character to the right; the new match pattern becomes T T T T. The whole process begins anew.

TF Listing

Here is the complete program:

```
1  '            TF, Vers. 2.2

100 '            Supervisor
110 GOSUB 190      ' Initialization
120 GOSUB 250      ' First LE inputs from player
130 GOSUB 310      ' Input
140 GOSUB 550      ' Printing and scorekeeping
150 GOSUB 380      ' Location update
160 GOSUB 490      ' Match-pattern update
170 GOSUB 420      ' Location calculation
180 GOTO 130
```

```
190 '          Initialization
200 RANDOM
210 DIM Q(1111, 2)
220 LE = 4
230 CLS
240 RETURN


250 '          First LE inputs from player
260 FOR I = 1 TO LE
270 GOSUB 310
280 MP(I) = CD
290 NEXT I
300 RETURN


310 '          Input
320 PRINT @ 625, "READY";
330 IP$ = INKEY$: IF IP$ = "T" OR IP$ = "F" THEN 340 ELSE 330
340 IF IP$ = "T" THEN CD = 1: GOTO 360
350 IF IP$ = "F" THEN CD = 0: GOTO 360
360 CLS
370 RETURN


380 '          Location update
390 IF CD = 1 THEN Q(LO, 1) = Q(LO, 1) + 1: GOTO 410
400 IF CD = 0 THEN Q(LO, 2) = Q(LO, 2) + 1
410 RETURN


420 '          Location calculation
430 A$ = ""
440 FOR I = 1 TO LE
450 A$ = A$ + MID$(STR$(MP(I)), 2)
460 NEXT I
470 LO = VAL(A$)
480 RETURN


490 '          Match-pattern update
500 FOR I = 1 TO LE - 1
510 MP(I) = MP(I + 1)
520 NEXT I
530 MP(LE) = CD
540 RETURN


550 '          Printing and scorekeeping
560 PRINT @ 384, "YOU TYPED:                      " IP$
570 PRINT @ 448, "COMPUTER WAS PREDICTING:"
580 IF Q(LO, 1) > Q(LO, 2) THEN TF$ = "T": T = T + 1:
    PRINT @ 480, TF$: GOTO 630
590 IF Q(LO, 2) > Q(LO, 1) THEN TF$ = "F": F = F + 1:
    PRINT @ 480, TF$: GOTO 630
600 RAN = RND(2)
610 IF RAN = 1 THEN TF$ = "T": T = T + 1: PRINT @ 480, TF$
620 IF RAN = 2 THEN TF$ = "F": F = F + 1: PRINT @ 480, TF$
630 IF TF$ = IP$ THEN NC = NC + 1
640 PRINT @ 512, "TOTAL NUMBER OF ENTRIES:        " T + F
650 PRINT @ 576, "NUMBER OF CORRECT PRE-"
660 PRINT @ 641, "DICTIONS BY THE COMPUTER:       " NC
670 PRINT @ 704, "PERCENT OF CORRECT PRE-"
680 PRINT @ 769, "DICTIONS BY THE COMPUTER:       "
    INT(((NC / (T + F)) * 100) * 10 + .5) / 10; "%"
690 RETURN
```

Possible Modifications

(1) Set variable LE (line 220) to 2 or 3 instead of 4. This alters the length of the match pattern and produces interesting results. If a match pattern longer than four letters (LE > 4) is desired, the program's data storage routines will have to be rewritten.

(2) If you happen to be familiar with any of the standard statistical tests of validity, you could try measuring TF's performance with one of these tests to see if the program actually has any predictive ability, and if so, how much.

(3) Connect your BASIC's random-number generator to the input subroutine (line 310) so that the value of IP$ is *truly* a random T or F. If this were done, it would be interesting to compare the results with the ones you got previously to see if there are any observable differences. You might also fix the output of the random-number generator in such a way that the output becomes a mixture of the two letters in the ratio of, for instance, 60 percent T to 40 percent F. TF will react markedly to such a lopsided output.

CHAPTER 4

Programs That Reason

This chapter will consider programs that perform automatic deductive question answering. Such programs are able to accept data which is input in the form of English sentences (although usually only a very limited subset of English is allowed), and, when asked questions about the data, respond with an appropriate answer in English. Furthermore, most question-answering programs are capable of making inferences, i.e., they are able to sort through the data which they have been given and find certain logical relationships between classes of data. The discovery of these logical relationships constitutes deductive reasoning.

Question-answering (Q/A) programs have been produced in great numbers in the last twenty years; there are probably dozens of existing programs which perform some type of deductive question answering. The main emphasis in this chapter will be on the reasoning ability of such programs. We will return to the subject of Q/A programs in Chapter 7, where we will be mainly interested in their natural-language processing capabilities.

SIR

A typical earlier Q/A program is Bertram Raphael's Semantic Information Retrieval (SIR), which was completed in 1964. Here is a portion of a conversation with SIR (uppercase and lowercase lines are the human input; lines with all capitals are the computer's responses):

```
Max is an IBM 7094.
I UNDERSTAND.
An IBM 7094 is a computer.
I UNDERSTAND.
Is Max a computer?
YES.
The boy is an MIT student.
I UNDERSTAND.
Every MIT student is a bright person.
I UNDERSTAND.
Is the boy a bright person?
YES.
```

The facts that Max is a computer and that the boy is a bright person are never explicitly stated by the human who is communicating with SIR. SIR had to draw these conclusions for itself.

How could a BASIC program be written which would duplicate some of the abilities of SIR? The task is actually not too difficult. But before we can get started on the programming, we must make a brief (very brief) excursion into the realm of logic.

The Hypothetical Syllogism

A *syllogism* is a short argument form. It consists of one or more *premises,* and a *conclusion* which is *inferred* or drawn from the premises. Here is a syllogism from the time of Aristotle:

```
Socrates is a man.
A man is mortal.
Therefore, Socrates is mortal.
```

The first two lines are the premises; the third is the conclusion. Notice that the conclusion, *Socrates is mortal,* does not contain any new empirical information. Given the two premises *Socrates is a man* and *A man is mortal,* it is not possible to deduce, for instance, that Socrates lectured at Athens or that he was forced to drink hemlock. The process of deductive reasoning cannot produce new empirical data. Deductive reasoning can only discover *relationships* between various classes of data, relationships that must be implicit in the premises of a given argument.

We can immediately see from the two premises above that *Socrates is mortal* is a valid conclusion. Why? Because this conclusion from these premises corresponds to a pattern which we unhesitatingly accept as a form of valid logical reasoning, namely, if A is B, and B is C, then A is C. A pattern whose conclusion must be true if its premises are true is called a *tautology.* It is unthinkable that a tautology could not be true, that is, that there could ever be a case where A is B and B is C, yet A is not C. Logicians refer to this particular tautology (there are many others, of course) as the *hypothetical syllogism*.

In the exchange with SIR quoted previously, the program applies the hypothetical syllogism twice to the data it was given in order to find a correct answer to the two questions that were asked. In the first instance, the program was given the data

Max is an IBM 7094.

and

An IBM 7094 is a computer.

from which it made the deduction

Max is a computer.

In the second instance it was given the data

The boy is an MIT student.

and

Every MIT student is a bright person.

from which it made the deduction

The boy is a bright person.

FETCH

Our BASIC program, FETCH, will store data and make deductions from this data based on the principle of the hypothetical syllogism. In addition, the program will be able to retrieve data on request, and it will work entirely in ordinary English (but in a severely limited subset of ordinary English).

Fig. 4-1 shows a video display of a computer running FETCH. In this illustration the lines preceded by a question mark are user inputs; the other lines are generated by the computer.

Supervisor

The FETCH supervisor controls six subroutines:

```
10 '          Supervisor
20 GOSUB 100     ' Initialization
30 GOSUB 160     ' Input
40 GOSUB 200     ' Determine where to send control
50 IF X = 1 THEN GOSUB 550    ' Interrogative sentences
60 IF X = 2 THEN GOSUB 830    ' Requests
70 IF X = 3 THEN GOSUB 290    ' Declarative sentences
80 GOTO 30
```

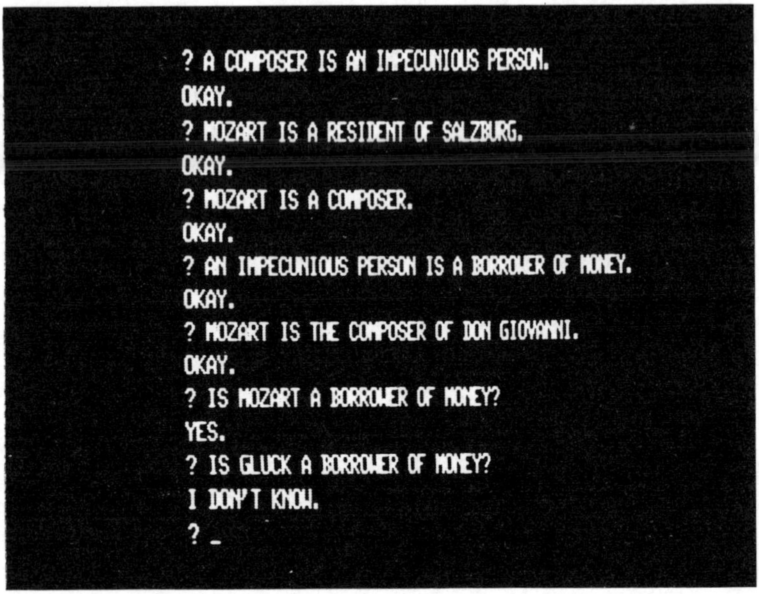

Fig. 4-1. Video display of computer running FETCH.

The initialization subroutine does the usual setting-up chores. The input subroutine allows the user to enter data and commands into the computer in the form of complete English sentences. These sentences are stored in variable DA$ (for "data sentence"). The sentences can be any one of three types: declarative, interrogative, and request.

(1) Declarative. This is how the user gives data to FETCH. Declarative sentences must be in the form:

noun/noun phrase—IS—noun/noun phrase—.

A noun could be, for instance, COMPUTER. Or the user can substitute a noun phrase, such as GREAT BIG COMPUTER WITH BLINKING LIGHTS. IS is just that. No other predicate is allowed. The sentence must end with a period. In addition, an article—A, AN, or THE—may appear before either of the nouns/noun phrases.

Here are two declarative sentences which follow this format:

SOCRATES IS A MAN.
STEVE'S HOMEBREW COMPUTER IS A 6809-BASED MACHINE.

(2) Interrogative. This is how the user gives commands to FETCH which may involve deduction. Interrogative sentences must be in this form:

IS—noun/noun phrase—article—noun/noun phrase—?

An article must appear before the second noun/noun phrase; the article is optional before the first. The question mark (or some other punctuation) is mandatory at the end of the sentence. For example:

IS STEVE'S HOMEBREW COMPUTER A 6809-BASED MACHINE?

(3) Requests. This is how the user retrieves large chunks of data from FETCH. Requests are not complete sentences; instead, they follow this simple format:

REQUEST—noun/noun phrase—.

No article is allowed before the noun or noun phrase when making a request. Example:

REQUEST SOCRATES.

The next subroutine (200) determines where to send program control. This subroutine checks the sentence contained in variable DA$. If the sentence begins with "IS " it is an interrogative sentence and X is assigned the value 1. If the sentence begins with "REQUEST " it is a request for data and X is set to 2. If the sentence contains " IS " (notice the difference between "IS " and " IS ") it is a declarative sentence and X is set to 3. If none of these conditions are satisfied, an input error has been committed. X is set to 4 and control returns to the input routine to allow the user another try.

Declarative Sentences

If X = 3, DA$ contains a declarative sentence and the supervisor passes the sentence on the subroutine at 290 for processing. Here is the subroutine:

```
290 '          Declarative sentences
300 '          A.  Parser
310 DL$ = LEFT$(DA$, I - 1): DR$ = MID$(DA$, I + 4)
320 FOR I = 1 TO 6
330 READ AR$
340 IF MID$(DL$, 1, LEN(AR$)) = AR$ THEN
    DL$ = MID$(DL$, LEN(AR$) + 1)
350 NEXT I
360 RESTORE
370 FOR I = 1 TO 6
380 READ AR$
390 IF MID$(DR$, 1, LEN(AR$)) = AR$ THEN
    DR$ = MID$(DR$, LEN(AR$) + 1)
400 NEXT I
410 RESTORE
420 DATA " A ", " AN ", " THE ", "A ", "AN ", "THE "
430 '          B.  Data storage
440 FOR I = 0 TO 9
450 IF A$(0, I) = DL$ THEN 500
460 NEXT I
470 FOR I = 0 TO 9
480 IF A$(0, I) = "X" THEN A$(0, I) = DL$: A$(0, I + 1) = "X":
    A$(1, I) = DR$: A$(2, I) = "X": GOTO 530
490 NEXT I
500 FOR J = 1 TO 9
510 IF A$(J, I) = "X" THEN A$(J, I) = DR$:
    A$(J + 1, I) = "X": GOTO 530
520 NEXT J
530 PRINT "OKAY."
540 RETURN
```

This subroutine is divided into two sections. The first section is
a *parser* and the second is concerned with data storage. Let's consider the parser first.

"Parse" is a term used by linguists to describe the analysis of a
sentence into subject, predicate, object, etc. The word has been
borrowed by computer people; in a computer context, "parse"
means to check any alphanumeric string that is input to a program for correct syntax. We will slightly extend the meaning of
the word so that a parser will be taken to be a routine which sepa-
rates any alphanumeric string into fields for purposes which may
include (but are not limited to) syntactic analysis.

The parser contained in lines 300–420 takes the declarative
sentence which the user has typed and divides it into two fields.
The portion of the sentence on the left side of the IS is placed into
DL$ ("data left") and the portion on the right is placed in DR$
("data right"). For instance, if the sentence "BASIC IS A COM-
PUTER LANGUAGE" were input, DL$ = "BASIC" and DR$ = "A
COMPUTER LANGUAGE." Notice that the object in DL$ is always
a subset of the object in DR$. Lines 320–420, which form the bulk
of the parsing routine, remove initial articles, if they are present,
from DL$ and DR$. So, in our example, DL$ remains "BASIC" but
DR$ becomes "COMPUTER LANGUAGE."

Next, the contents of DL$ and DR$ must be stored in a format which preserves their essential set-subset relationship. This can be accomplished using a storage structure no more complicated than a two-dimensional 9 × 9 array. In Microsoft BASIC a DIM statement is not required for a 9 × 9 array, but this limits the storage area to 100 items. If more storage space is needed, the program can be revised so that it will contain more data.

Lines 430–540 maintain the storage structure, which is string array A$. Fig. 4-2 is a graphic representation of part of the same array.

When the program is initialized, lines 130 and 140 set the entire top row of the array—A$(0, 0) through A$ (0, 9)—to the value "X", as illustrated in Fig. 4-3. The "X" is used as an end of column marker.

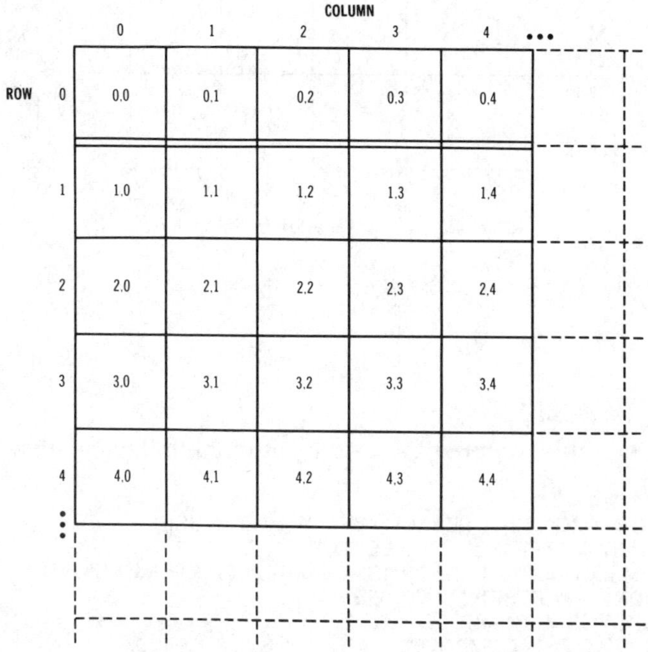

COLUMN

		0	1	2	3	4	...
ROW	0	0.0	0.1	0.2	0.3	0.4	
	1	1.0	1.1	1.2	1.3	1.4	
	2	2.0	2.1	2.2	2.3	2.4	
	3	3.0	3.1	3.2	3.3	3.4	
	4	4.0	4.1	4.2	4.3	4.4	

Fig. 4-2. A portion of the 9 × 9 array A$.

When the program is given a series of data statements, e.g., A is B, A is C, A is D, B is X, B is Y, B is Z, the data storage routine sorts them into columns, with the object being described at the top of the column and each of the classes of which it is a member arranged under it:

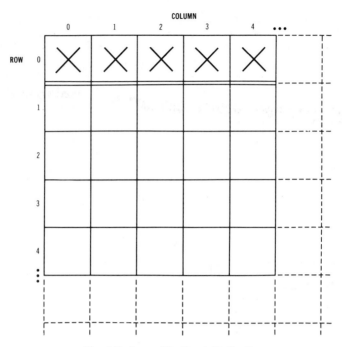

Fig. 4-3. Array A$ after initialization.

A	B
B	X
C	Y
D	Z

For example, suppose the user types in the following eight data items:

A COMPOSER IS A PERSON WHO WRITES MUSIC.
MOZART IS THE SON OF LEOPOLD.
AN IMPECUNIOUS PERSON IS A BORROWER OF MONEY.
HAYDN IS A RESIDENT OF VIENNA.
MOZART IS A COMPOSER.
HAYDN IS THE COMPOSER OF MANY SYMPHONIES.
A COMPOSER IS AN IMPECUNIOUS PERSON.
MOZART IS THE COMPOSER OF DON GIOVANNI.

For each of these sentences, the data storage routine takes DL$ (the noun or noun phrase that is on the left side of the IS) and looks for it in row 0. There are two possibilities:

(1) The routine does *not* find DL$ in row 0, in which case it puts DL$ at the *top* of the first available (unoccupied) column.

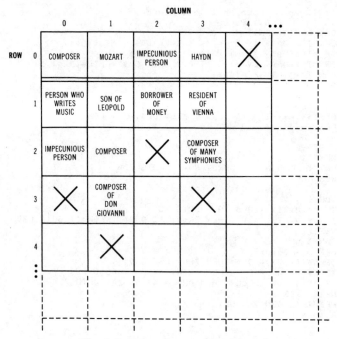

Fig. 4-4. Array after receiving data.

DR$ (the noun/noun phrase on the right side of the IS) is then placed in that same column just below DL$. The end of column marker "X" is placed below DR$.

(2) The routine *does* find DL$ in row 0, in which case it searches down the length of the column until it finds "X". The "X" is shoved one position down in the column and DR$ is placed in the position formerly occupied by "X".

The process can possibly be better understood by referring to Fig. 4-4. Fig. 4-4 illustrates the array once the eight data sentences above have been input to the program.

Interrogative Sentences

If X = 2, DA$ contains an interrogative sentence, and the supervisor calls the subroutine at 550 to deal with it:

```
550 '          Interrogative sentences
560 '               A.  Parser
570 DA$ = MID$(DA$, 4)
572 IF MID$(DA$, 1, 2) = "A " THEN DA$ = MID$(DA$, 3)
574 IF MID$(DA$, 1, 3) = "AN " THEN DA$ = MID$(DA$, 4)
576 IF MID$(DA$, 1, 4) = "THE " THEN DA$ = MID$(DA$, 5)
580 FOR I = 1 TO LEN(DA$)
590 FOR J = 1 TO 3
600 READ AR$
610 IF MID$(DA$, I, LEN(AR$)) = AR$ THEN DL$ =
  - LEFT$(DA$, I - 1): DR$ = MID$(DA$, I + LEN(AR$)):
    GOTO 660
620 NEXT J
630 RESTORE
640 NEXT I
650 PRINT "I DON'T UNDERSTAND.": GOTO 820
660 RESTORE
700 '               B.  Data retrieval
710 FOR I = 0 TO 9
720 IF A$(0, I) = DL$ THEN GOTO 750
730 IF A$(0, I) = "X" THEN PRINT "I DON'T KNOW.": GOTO 820
740 NEXT I
750 FOR I = 1 TO 9
760 FOR J = 0 TO 9
770 IF A$(I, J) = DR$ THEN 780 ELSE 800
780 IF A$(0, J) = DL$ THEN PRINT "YES.": GOTO 820
790 IF A$(0, J) <> DL$ THEN DR$ = A$(0, J): GOTO 750
800 NEXT J, I
810 PRINT "I DON'T KNOW."
820 RETURN
```

The parser in lines 560–660 prepares the essential data of the sentence to be matched against the data stored in array A$.

If DA$ = "IS HAYDN A RESIDENT OF VIENNA" (the question mark at the end of the sentence would have been removed by line 210) then line 570 rids the sentence of the initial "IS "; DA$ now contains "HAYDN A RESIDENT OF VIENNA." Lines 572–576 look for an article before "HAYDN"; if one is found, it is removed. Lines 580–660 split DA$ into two fields and remove the article which separates the fields, so DL$ = "HAYDN" and DR$ = "RESIDENT OF VIENNA."

The READ statement in line 600 gets its data from line 420. Looking at lines 580–660 you will notice that the routine has been arranged so that only the first three data items from line 420—the only ones that are needed—are ever read into variable AR$.

Now it is the task of the data retrieval routine at lines 700–820 to find the information that has been requested, if it exists. This is the portion of the program that makes deductions based on the hypothetical syllogism.

Let's assume the data of Fig. 4-4 has been input to the program and the question being asked is "IS MOZART A BORROWER OF MONEY?" Then DL$ = "MOZART" and DR$ = "BORROWER OF MONEY." The fact that Mozart is a borrower of money has never been explicitly given to FETCH. However, it is *implicitly* contained in these sentences which *were* input to the program:

```
MOZART IS A COMPOSER.
A COMPOSER IS AN IMPECUNIOUS PERSON.
AN IMPECUNIOUS PERSON IS A BORROWER OF MONEY.
```

from which the program ought to be able to draw the conclusion that Mozart is a borrower of money. Incidentally, it is, of course, blatantly false that a composer is always an impecunious person, or that an impecunious person is always a borrower of money. But we are not concerned here with the truth or falsity of the statements that we are feeding to FETCH, only with their logical consequences when assumed to be true.

How, then, does FETCH use the hypothetical syllogism to extract the desired conclusion from the data stored in the array? The data retrieval routine searches through row 0 of the array—A$(0, 0) to A$(0, 9)—looking for DL$ ("MOZART"). (The reader should refer to Fig. 4-4.) If it doesn't find it, then the program has no data on the subject of Mozart. "I DON'T KNOW" is printed, and control returns to the supervisor.

But if it *does* find "MOZART" at the top of one of the columns, this means that some data has been input on the subject of Mozart. Whether this is the data that is needed to answer the question, or this data must be deduced from other information in the table, or the data is simply not present in the table, is not known at this point. So the program (lines 750–800) proceeds by matching the contents of DR$ ("BORROWER OF MONEY") against each location in the table beginning with A$(1, 0). If "BORROWER OF MONEY" is found somewhere in the table, the program looks at the top of the column in which it was found. If the item at the top of the column is "MOZART," then the program prints "YES," since the question "IS MOZART A BORROWER OF MONEY?" has been found to be true. If "BORROWER OF MONEY" is nowhere to be found in the table, then "I DON'T KNOW" is printed, since Mozart may or may not be a borrower of money as far as the program knows.

But what about the case illustrated in Fig. 4-4, where "BORROWER OF MONEY" is located prominently in the table, but the data item at the top of the column is not "MOZART" but "IMPECUNIOUS PERSON"? This establishes that "BORROWER OF MONEY" is linked with "IMPECUNIOUS PERSON"; the program must now try to link "IMPECUNIOUS PERSON" with "MOZART." If it manages to do so, it will have performed the deduction necessary to answer the original question. So line 790 replaces the contents of DR$, "BORROWER OF MONEY," with "IMPECU-

NIOUS PERSON," and the matching process begins once again with location A$(1, 0) of the table.

Staying with the same example of Fig. 4-4, "IMPECUNIOUS PERSON" is located in column 0, but the data item at the top of the column is "COMPOSER." "IMPECUNIOUS PERSON" is replaced in DR$ by "COMPOSER"; matching begins again. The program finds "COMPOSER" in column 1, and this time the data item at the top of the column is "MOZART." The program therefore concludes that Mozart is indeed a borrower of money, and prints "YES" in response to the question.

Notice that in performing the deduction, FETCH works in reverse. It takes the data item, "BORROWER OF MONEY," and works backwards, step by step, until it manages to link it to "MOZART."

This method of automatic deduction that we have described has one serious weakness. When inputting data statements, if the property on the right side of the IS is used more than once, the deduction routine will become confused because the same data item will be contained in several different columns. For example, the sentences

MOZART IS THE COMPOSER OF DON GIOVANNI.
MOZART IS THE COMPOSER OF DIE ZAUBERFLOETE.
MOZART IS THE COMPOSER OF LE NOZZE DI FIGARO.

may all be typed in at the same time, since the property on the right side of the IS is different in each sentence. But the sentences

MOZART IS A CHILD PRODIGY.
MENDELSSOHN IS A CHILD PRODIGY.

cannot both be typed in during the same run of the program, or the deduction routine may go astray.

Requests

If X = 3, the input sentence is a request, and control passes to the subroutine at 830:

```
830 '          Requests
840 '          A.  Parser
850 DL$ = MID$(DA$, 9)
860 '          B.  Data retrieval
870 FOR I = 0 TO 9
880 IF A$(0, I) = DL$ THEN 910
890 NEXT I
900 PRINT "I HAVE NO DATA CONCERNING " DL$ ".": GOTO 960
910 PRINT DL$ " IS--"
920 FOR J = 1 TO 9
930 IF A$(J, I) = "X" THEN 960
940 PRINT A$(J, I)
950 NEXT J
960 RETURN
```

Line 850 is a one-line parser which simply removes the initial word of the request and the blank which follows it. If the request is "REQUEST MOZART," DL$ = "MOZART" after 850.

Lines 860–960 look for DL$ in row 0 of the table. If DL$ cannot be located, the program prints "I HAVE NO DATA CONCERNING" followed by DL$ followed by a period. If DL$ *is* located, the contents of each location in the column below it are printed until the end of column marker is reached.

A request causes all data for a data item to be printed. This is useful when the user wants to see all the information that has been stored in connection with a certain data item. Requests, however, are not deductive; only the data that has been explicitly assigned to the data item will be printed.

Assuming once again the data of Fig. 4-4, here is an example of what FETCH does when it receives a request:

```
? REQUEST MOZART.
MOZART IS—
SON OF LEOPOLD
COMPOSER
COMPOSER OF DON GIOVANNI
? REQUEST COMPOSER.
COMPOSER IS—
PERSON WHO WRITES MUSIC
IMPECUNIOUS PERSON
? REQUEST BOCCHERINI.
I HAVE NO DATA CONCERNING BOCCHERINI.
```

FETCH Listing

Here is the complete listing for FETCH:

```
1 '          FETCH, Vers. 3.1
2 CLEAR 500


10 '          Supervisor
20 GOSUB 100       ' Initialization
30 GOSUB 160       ' Input
40 GOSUB 200       ' Determine where to send control
50 IF X = 1 THEN GOSUB 550       ' Interrogative sentences
60 IF X = 2 THEN GOSUB 830       ' Requests
70 IF X = 3 THEN GOSUB 290       ' Declarative sentences
80 GOTO 30


100 '          Initialization
110 CLS
120 FOR I = 0 TO 9
130 A$(0, I) = "X"
140 NEXT I
150 RETURN
```

```
160 '            Input
170 X = 0
180 INPUT DA$
190 RETURN


200 '          Determine where to send control
210 DA$ = LEFT$(DA$, LEN(DA$) - 1)
220 IF MID$(DA$, 1, 3) = "IS " THEN X = 1: GOTO 280
230 IF MID$(DA$, 1, 8) = "REQUEST " THEN X = 2: GOTO 280
240 FOR I = 1 TO LEN(DA$)
250 IF MID$(DA$, I, 4) = " IS " THEN X = 3: GOTO 280
260 NEXT I
270 X = 4
280 RETURN



290 '            Declarative sentences
300 '          A. Parser
310 DL$ = LEFT$(DA$, I - 1): DR$ = MID$(DA$, I + 4)
320 FOR I = 1 TO 6
330 READ AR$
340 IF MID$(DL$, 1, LEN(AR$)) = AR$ THEN
    DL$ = MID$(DL$, LEN(AR$) + 1)
350 NEXT I
360 RESTORE
370 FOR I = 1 TO 6
380 READ AR$
390 IF MID$(DR$, 1, LEN(AR$)) = AR$ THEN
    DR$ = MID$(DR$, LEN(AR$) + 1)
400 NEXT I
410 RESTORE
420 DATA " A ", " AN ", " THE ", "A ", "AN ", "THE "
430 '          B. Data storage
440 FOR I = 0 TO 9
450 IF A$(0, I) = DL$ THEN 500
460 NEXT I
470 FOR I = 0 TO 9
480 IF A$(0, I) = "X" THEN A$(0, I) = DL$: A$(0, I + 1) = "X":
    A$(1, I) = DR$: A$(2, I) = "X": GOTO 530
490 NEXT I
500 FOR J = 1 TO 9
510 IF A$(J, I) = "X" THEN A$(J, I) = DR$:
    A$(J + 1, I) = "X": GOTO 530
520 NEXT J
530 PRINT "OKAY."
540 RETURN



550 '            Interrogative sentences
560 '          A. Parser
570 DA$ = MID$(DA$, 4)
572 IF MID$(DA$, 1, 2) = "A " THEN DA$ = MID$(DA$, 3)
574 IF MID$(DA$, 1, 3) = "AN " THEN DA$ = MID$(DA$, 4)
576 IF MID$(DA$, 1, 4) = "THE " THEN DA$ = MID$(DA$, 5)
580 FOR I = 1 TO LEN(DA$)
590 FOR J = 1 TO 3
600 READ AR$
610 IF MID$(DA$, I, LEN(AR$)) = AR$ THEN DL$ =
    LEFT$(DA$, I - 1): DR$ = MID$(DA$, I + LEN(AR$)):
    GOTO 660
```

```
620 NEXT J
630 RESTORE
640 NEXT I
650 PRINT "I DON'T UNDERSTAND.": GOTO 820
660 RESTORE
700 '          B.  Data retrieval
710 FOR I = 0 TO 9
720 IF A$(0, I) = DL$ THEN GOTO 750
730 IF A$(0, I) = "X" THEN PRINT "I DON'T KNOW.": GOTO 820
740 NEXT I
750 FOR I = 1 TO 9
760 FOR J = 0 TO 9
770 IF A$(I, J) = DR$ THEN 780 ELSE 800
780 IF A$(0, J) = DL$ THEN PRINT "YES.": GOTO 820
790 IF A$(0, J) <> DL$ THEN DR$ = A$(0, J): GOTO 75,0
800 NEXT J, I
810 PRINT "I DON'T KNOW."
820 RETURN


830 '          Requests
840 '          A.  Parser
850 DL$ = MID$(DA$, 9)
860 '          B.  Data retrieval
870 FOR I = 0 TO 9
880 IF A$(0, I) = DL$ THEN 910
890 NEXT I
900 PRINT "I HAVE NO DATA CONCERNING " DL$ ".": GOTO 960
910 PRINT DL$ " IS--"
920 FOR J = 1 TO 9
930 IF A$(J, I) = "X" THEN 960
940 PRINT A$(J, I)
950 NEXT J
960 RETURN
```

Possible Modifications

FETCH as presented above is a sort of skeleton program. While FETCH is interesting to play with just as it is, it can be expanded and its utility increased in any number of ways. Here are two suggestions:

(1) You may want to try increasing the deductive abilities of FETCH so that it is able to reason using logic in addition to the hypothetical syllogism. A book on traditional or symbolic logic would be very helpful. Bertram Raphael, author of the program SIR (of which FETCH is a much-simplified version), says that it was hard to extend the capabilities of SIR because the programming became too difficult. However, it will take substantial changes before FETCH reaches quite that level of complexity.

(2) It would be useful to save the data contained in FETCH on cassette or diskette so that it could be stored for long periods and retrieved when needed. This project becomes feasible if your BASIC has input/output statements which allow data to be written to mass memory.

CHAPTER 5

Computer Verse

This chapter and the next deal with computer simulation of the creative process. In this chapter a program is developed which composes poetry. In Chapter 6 a program which writes simple stories is examined. But, first, it may be helpful to think about how the creative process occurs in the human mind. This knowledge will give us a hint as to the most effective method of simulating or duplicating creativity in a computer program.

The question of the nature of creativity is not an easy one; it has occupied thoughtful people probably since the dawn of civilization. One possibility is that the creative process is based on the interplay of ideas in the human mind, that is, the ability to be reminded by object A or concept A of some other object or concept that may be only peripherally related to A. For instance, while looking at a group of stars one shepherd sees only stars; another shepherd is reminded of a head, shoulders, legs, a sword hanging from a belt. . .and names the stars "Orion."

In this chapter we will see how a program can be written which composes poetry by forcing concept A into close association with concept B. The reader of the poem will often be able to make a connection between the two concepts and perceive meaning within the poem as a whole.

The Haiku

The poet has a great amount of latitude when writing poetry and is free to position words and phrases in unfamiliar and sometimes strikingly unusual ways. This is particularly true of the type of poetry which our program will generate, namely, those short poems known as *haiku*. The haiku originated in Japan about four centuries ago, and today it is the most popular form of poetry in the world.

In its most classical version, the haiku consists of three lines, with five syllables in the first line, seven syllables in the second, and five in the third. The aim of haiku poets is to extract the *essence* of a deeply felt moment and cast it into haiku form. Haiku poets are also fond of using natural images as metaphors for human feelings and behavior.

HAIKU

Our haiku-composing program will be called, fittingly enough, HAIKU. HAIKU has a built-in vocabulary of 124 words, making it unnecessary for the user to key in words when the program is run.

Fig. 5-1. Video display of computer running HAIKU.

On the other hand, the vocabulary can easily be expanded or changed to make the program compose using whatever set of words is desired. A new poem is generated every time the carriage return is pressed; the haiku is printed line by line on the display as it is composed. As you can see from Fig. 5-1 and the following four poems, HAIKU is capable of some rather fanciful imagery in the poems it creates.

THE BITTER WITHERED MOUNTAIN;
UNDER THE QUIET SHAPE
A SURF FLUTTERS

A DARK FEATHER IS FLOATING;
THE LINGERING ICY MOON
THROUGH AN AZURE NIGHT

A SPRING MEADOW . . .
THE MOON SLEEPS UNDER A BUSH
BROKEN BLUE SNOWFLAKE

PINE IN THE SUN;
A SPARKLING FIREFLY IN THE HILL
FALLING RIVER

If you count, you will find that not one of the poems above and in Fig. 5-1 has five syllables in the first line, seven in the second, and five in the third. Modern poets who work in this form rarely limit themselves to the classical 5-7-5 pattern of syllables. And in any case this procedure is structured to the Japanese language and not particularly suited to English, since the *jion* or Japanese syllable-sound is not equivalent to the English syllable. Accordingly, the poems which HAIKU creates are not limited to the 5-7-5 pattern.

Supervisor

The HAIKU supervisor controls seven subroutines:

```
10 '          Supervisor
20 GOSUB 120      ' Initialization
30 GOTO 50
40 GOSUB 200      ' Input
50 GOSUB 260      ' Determine haiku pattern
60 IF RAN = 1 THEN GOSUB 450     ' First haiku pattern
70 IF RAN = 2 THEN GOSUB 670     ' Second haiku pattern
80 IF RAN = 3 THEN GOSUB 890     ' Third haiku pattern
90 IF RAN = 4 THEN GOSUB 1110    ' Fourth haiku pattern
100 GOTO 40
```

Subroutine 120 performs the usual initialization tasks. When the program has finished printing a poem on the screen, subroutine 200 causes program execution to be suspended until the user types a carriage return; a new program will then be generated and printed.

Which Pattern?

This brings us to the heart of the program. Subroutines 450, 670, 890, and 1110 contain four *haiku patterns* which are used by the program as a framework for the creation of its own poems. These patterns, which were extracted from actual poems, represent the syntactic skeletons of four different haiku. Subroutine 260 generates a random number between 1 and 4. Depending on the number that is produced, control passes to one of the subroutines 450, 670, 890, or 1110.

First Haiku Pattern

Let's dissect one of these pattern subroutines:

```
450 '          First haiku pattern
460 N = ARTNMB: P = 0: GOSUB 380
470 N = ADJNMB: P = ARTNMB: GOSUB 380
480 N = NOUNNMB: P = ARTNMB + ADJNMB: GOSUB 380
490 GOSUB 300
500 LIN$ =LIN$ + "..."
510 PRINT @ 340, LIN$
520 LIN$ = ""
530 N = ARTNMB: P = 0: GOSUB 380
540 N = NOUNNMB: P = ARTNMB + ADJNMB: GOSUB 380
550 N = VERBNMB: P = ARTNMB + ADJNMB + NOUNNMB: GOSUB 380
560 N = PREPNMB: P = ARTNMB + ADJNMB + NOUNNMB + VERBNMB:
      GOSUB 380
570 N = ARTNMB: P = 0: GOSUB 380
580 N = NOUNNMB: P = ARTNMB + ADJNMB: GOSUB 380
590 GOSUB 300
600 PRINT @ 406, LIN$
610 LIN$ = ""
620 N = ADJNMB: P = ARTNMB: GOSUB 380
630 GOSUB 380
640 N = NOUNNMB: P = ARTNMB + ADJNMB: GOSUB 380
650 PRINT @ 472, LIN$
660 RETURN
```

The syntactic structure behind the first haiku pattern is

Article—adjective—noun—. . .
Article—noun—verb—preposition—article—noun
Adjective—adjective—noun

The subroutine needs an article, an adjective, and a noun to make up the first line of the poem. It selects an article, adjective, and noun at random from the vocabulary, adds the punctuation ". . .", and prints the line on the display. Then it moves on to the composition of the second line.

To see exactly how the subroutine determines the first line of the poem, look at lines 460–520. To begin with, the subroutine must get an article from the vocabulary. Line 460 sets N to

ARTNMB, the number of articles in the vocabulary. Since ARTNMB was set to 4 back in line 140, indicating that the vocabulary contains four articles (actually there are only three, "a," "an," and "the," but "the" is included twice to prevent a disproportionately large number of a's and an's from appearing in the poems), N is also assigned the value 4. Pointer value P is set to 0 in line 460, and subroutine 380 is called:

```
380 '          Choose words of poem
385 RAN = RND(N) + P
390 FOR I = 1 TO RAN
400 READ WRD$
410 NEXT I
420 LIN$ = LIN$ + " " + WRD$
430 RESTORE
440 RETURN
```

Subroutine 380 generates a random number between 1 and N and to this value adds the value of P. Let's say the number generated is 3. Now, $3 + 0 = 3$, so lines 390–410 read the third data item from the vocabulary, which is the article "AN," and line 420 places the word in variable LIN$, which contains the line being composed.

Control returns to line 470. The subroutine has gotten an article and now needs an adjective. N is set to ADJNMB; ADJNMB was set to 50 during initialization. P is set to ARTNMB, which is 4. P is being used as a pointer value, which enables the program to skip over whole sections of the vocabulary so that the word ultimately selected by the program will be the required part of speech. The subroutine at 380 is called again; a random number between 1 and N is generated. Since N is 50, the number generated may be anywhere between 1 and 50. Let's say the number is 2. Now P is added. Since P is 4, the resulting value is 6. The sixth data item, the adjective "HIDDEN," will be read from the vocabulary. The addition of P prevents the program from choosing an article when an adjective is needed.

Line 420 causes the word "HIDDEN" plus a blank to be concatenated to the value already in LIN$. So LIN$ now contains the value " AN HIDDEN."

Control returns again to the original subroutine, this time at line 480. Line 480 picks a noun at random from the vocabulary in the same fashion as just described; let's say the noun chosen is "MEADOW." So when control returns to line 490, LIN$ = " AN HIDDEN MEADOW."

The article "AN" is obviously not in agreement with the adjective "HIDDEN"; line 490 is designed to correct this situation. Line 490 calls the article-checking subroutine at 300:

```
300 '       Check articles
305 FOR I = 1 TO LEN(LIN$) - 2
010 IF MID$(LIN$, I, 3) = " A " THEN B$ = MID$(LIN$, I + 3, 1):
    IF B$ = "A" OR B$ = "E" OR B$ = "I" OR B$ = "O" OR B$ = "U"
    THEN LIN$ = LEFT$(LIN$, I + 1) + "N" + MID$(LIN$, I + 2)
320 NEXT I
330 FOR I = 1 TO LEN(LIN$) - 2
340 IF MID$(LIN$, I, 4) = " AN " THEN B$ =
    MID$(LIN$, I + 4, 1): IF B$ = "A" OR B$ = "E" OR B$ = "I"
    OR B$ = "O" OR B$ = "U" THEN 350 ELSE LIN$ =
    LEFT$(LIN$, I + 1) + MID$(LIN$, I + 3)
350 NEXT I
360 RETURN
```

This subroutine scans through the line of verse just composed. If it finds " A " before a vowel, or " AN " before a consonant, it converts the article to its proper form. When the article-checking subroutine has completed its work, LIN$ contains "A HIDDEN MEADOW."

Control now goes to line 500, which adds the punctuation ". . ." to the end of LIN$. Line 510 prints LIN$ on the screen:

A HIDDEN MEADOW. . .

Lines 530–660 generate the second and third lines of the haiku. The second, third, and fourth haiku patterns (subroutines 670, 890, and 1110) operate in a similar fashion.

Program Speed

The present version of HAIKU takes about 5 to 10 seconds to compose a poem, depending on how fast the BASIC in which it's written is. The speed of the program could be increased considerably, however, to the point where a new poem is printed on the screen instantly, as soon as the carriage return is pressed. This could be done by reading the entire vocabulary into several string arrays when the program is first initialized; when it's time to generate a poem the program simply prints out random elements from the appropriate arrays. In contrast, HAIKU requires a large portion of the vocabulary to be sorted through for each word incorporated into the poem; this sorting process consumes time.

But—given a fairly small vocabulary—the consumption of time is actually of benefit to the program. If each haiku is printed out immediately as soon as the carriage return is pressed, an observer soon begins to feel that the program is coming up with poems effortlessly, without thought or *creativity*, and the effect is spoiled.

The present version of HAIKU, which prints the poems line by line as they are generated and takes a few seconds to generate each line, eliminates this difficulty to some degree.

But it should be noted that the vocabulary of HAIKU is only 124 words. If the vocabulary begins to get lengthy, the program will take too long to generate individual poems, and the second approach—storing the entire vocabulary in arrays when the program is initialized—should be taken.

Let's take a look at the vocabulary of HAIKU:

```
2000 '          Program vocabulary
2010 '          A. Articles
2020 DATA A, THE, AN, THE
2030 '          B. Adjectives
2040 DATA AUTUMN, HIDDEN, BITTER, MISTY, SILENT, EMPTY
2050 DATA DRY, DARK, SUMMER, ICY, DELICATE, QUIET
2060 DATA WHITE, COOL, SPRING, WINTER, DAPPLED
2070 DATA TWILIGHT, DAWN, CRIMSON, WISPY, AZURE
2080 DATA BLUE, BILLOWING, BROKEN, COLD, DAMP, FALLING
2090 DATA FROSTY, GREEN, LONG, LATE, LINGERING, LIMPID
2100 DATA LITTLE, MORNING, MUDDY, OLD, RED, ROUGH
2110 DATA STILL, SMALL, SPARKLING, THROBBING, VERMILION
2120 DATA WANDERING, WITHERED, WILD, BLACK, YOUNG
2130 '          C. Nouns
2140 DATA WATERFALL, RIVER, BREEZE, MOON
2150 DATA RAIN, WIND, SEA, MORNING, SNOW, LAKE, SUNSET
2160 DATA PINE, SHADOW, LEAF, DAWN, GLITTER, FOREST
2170 DATA HILL, CLOUD, MEADOW, SUN, GLADE, BIRD, BROOK
2180 DATA BUTTERFLY, BUSH, DEW, DUST, FIELD, FIR
2190 DATA FLOWER, FIREFLY, FEATHER, GRASS, HAZE, MOUNTAIN
2200 DATA NIGHT, POND, SHADE, SNOWFLAKE
2210 DATA SILENCE, SOUND, SKY, SHAPE, SURF, THUNDER
2220 DATA VIOLET, WATER, WILDFLOWER, WAVE
2230 '          D. Verbs
2240 DATA SHAKES, DRIFTS, HAS STOPPED, STRUGGLES
2250 DATA HAS FALLEN, HAS PASSED, SLEEPS, CREEPS
2260 DATA FLUTTERS, HAS RISEN, IS FALLING, IS TRICKLING
2270 DATA MURMURS, IS FLOATING
2280 '          E. Prepositions
2290 DATA ON, IN, OF, UNDER, OVER, NEAR
```

This vocabulary was selected almost entirely from two volumes of haiku.* The selection process was very careful; the more painstakingly the vocabulary is assembled, the better (and more pertinent) the resulting poems will be.

The vocabulary can be altered or expanded by inserting new data lines in the appropriate sections. For example, if you want to add 10 nouns to the 50 already contained in lines 2130–2220, just insert two data lines containing the new nouns between lines 2220 and 2230, and change the value of variable NOUNNMB (line 160) to 60.

---

*H. G. Henderson, An Introduction to Haiku, Doubleday Anchor, 1958; C. van den Heuvel, The Haiku Anthology, Doubleday Anchor, 1974.

HAIKU Listing

Below is a complete listing of the program.

```
1 '            HAIKU, Vers. 1.2
2 CLEAR 200

10 '            Supervisor
20 GOSUB 120       ' Initialization
30 GOTO 50
40 GOSUB 200       ' Input
50 GOSUB 260       ' Determine haiku pattern
60 IF RAN = 1 THEN GOSUB 450      ' First haiku pattern
70 IF RAN = 2 THEN GOSUB 670      ' Second haiku pattern
80 IF RAN = 3 THEN GOSUB 890      ' Third haiku pattern
90 IF RAN = 4 THEN GOSUB 1110     ' Fourth haiku pattern
100 GOTO 40

120 '            Initialization
125 CLS
130 RANDOM
140 ARTNMB = 4
150 ADJNMB = 50
160 NOUNNMB = 50
170 VERBNMB = 14
180 PREPNMB = 6
190 RETURN

200 '            Input
210 LIN$ = ""
220 RESTORE
230 A$ = INKEY$: IF A$ = CHR$(13) THEN 240 ELSE 230
240 CLS
250 RETURN

260 '            Determine haiku pattern
270 RAN = RND(4)
280 RETURN

300 '            Check articles
305 FOR I = 1 TO LEN(LIN$) - 2
310 IF MID$(LIN$, I, 3) = " A " THEN B$ = MID$(LIN$, I + 3, 1):
    IF B$ = "A" OR B$ = "E" OR B$ = "I" OR B$ = "O" OR B$ = "U"
    THEN LIN$ = LEFT$(LIN$, I + 1) + "N" + MID$(LIN$, I + 2)
320 NEXT I
330 FOR I = 1 TO LEN(LIN$) - 2
340 IF MID$(LIN$, I, 4) = " AN " THEN B$ =
    MID$(LIN$, I + 4, 1): IF B$ = "A" OR B$ = "E" OR B$ = "I"
    OR B$ = "O" OR B$ = "U" THEN 350 ELSE LIN$ =
    LEFT$(LIN$, I + 1) + MID$(LIN$, I + 3)
350 NEXT I
360 RETURN

380 '            Choose words of poem
385 RAN = RND(N) + P
390 FOR I = 1 TO RAN
400 READ WRD$
410 NEXT I
420 LIN$ = LIN$ + " " + WRD$
430 RESTORE
440 RETURN
```

```
450 '          First haiku pattern
460 N = ARTNMB: P = 0: GOSUB 380
470 N = ADJNMB: P = ARTNMB: GOSUB 380
480 N = NOUNNMB: P = ARTNMB + ADJNMB: GOSUB 380
490 GOSUB 300
500 LIN$ =LIN$ + "..."
510 PRINT @ 340, LIN$
520 LIN$ = ""
530 N = ARTNMB: P = 0: GOSUB 380
540 N = NOUNNMB: P = ARTNMB + ADJNMB: GOSUB 380
550 N = VERBNMB: P = ARTNMB + ADJNMB + NOUNNMB: GOSUB 380
560 N = PREPNMB: P = ARTNMB + ADJNMB + NOUNNMB + VERBNMB:
    GOSUB 380
570 N = ARTNMB: P = 0: GOSUB 380
580 N = NOUNNMB: P = ARTNMB + ADJNMB: GOSUB 380
590 GOSUB 300
600 PRINT @ 406, LIN$
610 LIN$ = ""
620 N = ADJNMB: P = ARTNMB: GOSUB 380
630 GOSUB 380
640 N = NOUNNMB: P = ARTNMB + ADJNMB: GOSUB 380
650 PRINT @ 472, LIN$
660 RETURN

670 '          Second haiku pattern
680 N = NOUNNMB: P = ARTNMB + ADJNMB: GOSUB 380
690 N = PREPNMB: P = ARTNMB + ADJNMB + NOUNNMB + VERBNMB:
    GOSUB 380
700 N = ARTNMB: P = 0: GOSUB 380
710 N = NOUNNMB: P = ARTNMB + ADJNMB: GOSUB 380
720 GOSUB 300
730 LIN$ = LIN$ + ";"
740 PRINT @ 340, LIN$
750 LIN$ = ""
760 N = ARTNMB: P = 0: GOSUB 380
770 N = ADJNMB: P = ARTNMB: GOSUB 380
780 N = NOUNNMB: P = ARTNMB + ADJNMB: GOSUB 380
790 N = PREPNMB: P = ARTNMB + ADJNMB + NOUNNMB + VERBNMB:
    GOSUB 380
800 N = ARTNMB: P = 0: GOSUB 380
810 N = NOUNNMB: P = ARTNMB + ADJNMB: GOSUB 380
820 GOSUB 300
830 PRINT @ 406, LIN$
840 LIN$ = ""
850 N = ADJNMB: P = ARTNMB: GOSUB 380
860 N = NOUNNMB: P = ARTNMB + ADJNMB: GOSUB 380
870 PRINT @ 472, LIN$
880 RETURN

890 '          Third haiku pattern
900 N = ARTNMB: P = 0: GOSUB 380
910 N = ADJNMB: P = ARTNMB: GOSUB 380
920 GOSUB 380
930 N = NOUNNMB: P = ARTNMB + ADJNMB: GOSUB 380
940 GOSUB 300
950 LIN$ = LIN$ + ";"
960 PRINT @ 340, LIN$
970 LIN$ = ""
980 N = PREPNMB: P = ARTNMB + ADJNMB + NOUNNMB + VERBNMB:
    GOSUB 380
990 N = ARTNMB: P = 0: GOSUB 380
1000 N = ADJNMB: P = ARTNMB: GOSUB 380
1010 N = NOUNNMB: P = ARTNMB + ADJNMB: GOSUB 380
1020 GOSUB 300
```

```
1030 PRINT @ 406, LIN$
1040 LIN$ = ""
1050 N = ARTNMB: P = 0: GOSUB 380
1060 N = NOUNNMB: P = ARTNMB + ADJNMB: GOSUB 380
1070 N = VERBNMB: P = ARTNMB + ADJNMB + NOUNNMB: GOSUB 380
1080 GOSUB 300
1090 PRINT @ 472, LIN$
1100 RETURN

1110 '          Fourth haiku pattern
1120 N = ARTNMB: P = 0: GOSUB 380
1130 N = ADJNMB: P = ARTNMB: GOSUB 380
1140 N = NOUNNMB: P = ARTNMB + ADJNMB: GOSUB 380
1150 N = VERBNMB: P = ARTNMB + ADJNMB + NOUNNMB: GOSUB 380
1160 GOSUB 300
1170 LIN$ = LIN$ + ";"
1180 PRINT @ 340, LIN$
1190 LIN$ = ""
1200 N = ARTNMB: P = 0: GOSUB 380
1210 N = ADJNMB: P = ARTNMB: GOSUB 380
1220 GOSUB 380
1230 N = NOUNNMB: P = ARTNMB + ADJNMB: GOSUB 380
1240 GOSUB 300
1250 PRINT @ 406, LIN$
1260 LIN$ = ""
1270 N = PREPNMB: P = ARTNMB + ADJNMB + NOUNNMB + VERBNMB:
     GOSUB 380
1280 N = ARTNMB: P = 0: GOSUB 380
1290 N = ADJNMB: P = ARTNMB: GOSUB 380
1300 N = NOUNNMB: P = ARTNMB + ADJNMB: GOSUB 380
1310 GOSUB 300
1320 PRINT @ 472, LIN$
1330 RETURN

2000 '          Program vocabulary
2010 '          A. Articles
2020 DATA A, THE, AN, THE
2030 '          B. Adjectives
2040 DATA AUTUMN, HIDDEN, BITTER, MISTY, SILENT, EMPTY
2050 DATA DRY, DARK, SUMMER, ICY, DELICATE, QUIET
2060 DATA WHITE, COOL, SPRING, WINTER, DAPPLED
2070 DATA TWILIGHT, DAWN, CRIMSON, WISPY, AZURE
2080 DATA BLUE, BILLOWING, BROKEN, COLD, DAMP, FALLING
2090 DATA FROSTY, GREEN, LONG, LATE, LINGERING, LIMPID
2100 DATA LITTLE, MORNING, MUDDY, OLD, RED, ROUGH
2110 DATA STILL, SMALL, SPARKLING, THROBBING, VERMILION
2120 DATA WANDERING, WITHERED, WILD, BLACK, YOUNG
2130 '          C. Nouns
2140 DATA WATERFALL, RIVER, BREEZE, MOON
2150 DATA RAIN, WIND, SEA, MORNING, SNOW, LAKE, SUNSET
2160 DATA PINE, SHADOW, LEAF, DAWN, GLITTER, FOREST
2170 DATA HILL, CLOUD, MEADOW, SUN, GLADE, BIRD, BROOK
2180 DATA BUTTERFLY, BUSH, DEW, DUST, FIELD, FIR
2190 DATA FLOWER, FIREFLY, FEATHER, GRASS, HAZE, MOUNTAIN
2200 DATA NIGHT, POND, SHADE, SNOWFLAKE
2210 DATA SILENCE, SOUND, SKY, SHAPE, SURF, THUNDER
2220 DATA VIOLET, WATER, WILDFLOWER, WAVE
2230 '          D. Verbs
2240 DATA SHAKES, DRIFTS, HAS STOPPED, STRUGGLES
2250 DATA HAS FALLEN, HAS PASSED, SLEEPS, CREEPS
2260 DATA FLUTTERS, HAS RISEN, IS FALLING, IS TRICKLING
2270 DATA MURMURS, IS FLOATING
2280 '          E. Prepositions
2290 DATA ON, IN, OF, UNDER, OVER, NEAR
```

Possible Modifications

As was the case with last chapter's FETCH program, HAIKU presents the interested reader with numerous opportunities for tinkering.

The possibility of altering the vocabulary of the program was mentioned previously; here are some further suggestions for refinements:

(1) It would be an interesting challenge to modify the program in such a way that it produced haiku which were all built around the classical 5-7-5 pattern of syllables. A way of doing this which immediately suggests itself would be to include as program data the number of syllables contained in each word of the vocabulary, along with the vocabulary itself. From there it would be a simple job to write a subroutine which keeps track of the number of syllables in a line as it is composed and does not allow lines with more than the requisite number of syllables. If the last word chosen for the line has too many syllables so that consequently the resulting line is too long, the subroutine would throw that word out and look for another which does have the right number of syllables.

(2) The program as written has a somewhat annoying weakness: the same noun or adjective sometimes appears twice (or even more often) in the same poem. In some instances this is of little consequence because the repetition of the word will be meaningful given the context of the poem. Furthermore, the chance that the same word will be chosen more than once in the same poem decreases as the size of the vocabulary increases. In spite of this, however, occasionally HAIKU will come up with a poem like the following one:

> A LINGERING STILL SILENCE;
> ON THE LINGERING FOREST
> A SILENCE IS FALLING

This repetition of words can be avoided. For each haiku, all the values of RAN produced by the word-choosing subroutine (lines 370–440) can be stored. (RAN is the variable that points to the next word to be incorporated into the haiku.) Now, whenever the word-choosing subroutine generates a new value for RAN, this value is compared to the values of RAN that were previously stored. If the new value is equal to any of the old values, instead of incorporating the associated word into the poem, the word-choosing subroutine is called again. Exception has to be made for RAN <= 4, since these four values refer to the articles "a," "an," and "the."

(3) The *syntax* of a poem, that is, the types of words (nouns, verbs, etc.) contained in the poem and the placement of these words within the poem, is governed by the four subroutines which determine the haiku patterns. However, the *semantic* content of a poem, that is, its *meaning*, is determined by the words which are randomly chosen to fill the preassigned slots. The key point to notice here is that this process is a *random one*. Naturally, the human poet who composes a haiku exercises his best critical judgment as to which of concepts *X, Y,* or *Z* should be compared to concept *A,* or which of adjectives *x, y,* or *z* should modify noun *a.* HAIKU in its present form does no such thing; it chooses from among alternatives of this type not by exercising any sort of critical judgment, but by making a random selection. Thus the semantic content of the poems generated by HAIKU is bound to suffer. All too frequently the program will produce a line like

BREEZE OF THE SHAPE

which is clearly meaningless. HAIKU simply does not have the judgment necessary to realize that the noun "breeze" cannot be matched in a meaningful way with the prepositional phrase "of the shape."

The reader who doesn't mind tackling a difficult project is invited to try to improve the semantic content of the poems produced by HAIKU. One approach would be to divide all the words contained in the vocabulary into various categories; certain categories would never be allowed to interact with other categories, so that the program would be forbidden to ever match "breeze" with a prepositional phrase whose object is "shape." If you decide to try this word-categorization technique, be sure to start with a small vocabulary!

This method would doubtless enormously improve the quality of the output, but the objection could be raised that this is like giving the poem to the program already half-written. If so, another approach, a highly ambitious one, might be attempted. For each word in the vocabulary the program would be given certain data about the word. For instance, if one of the words was "red," the additional data would be supplied that "red" is an adjective, and that it specifies a color. If another of the words were "thought," the data would be supplied that "thought" is a noun and that it is an abstract noun (in contrast to a noun that is an object, like "table"). The program would also have a built-in set of rules that tell it what sort of word combinations to avoid; one of these rules would be that it must never use an adjective which specifies a color to modify an abstract noun, causing it to avoid a phrase like "red thought." Thus the program would be able to tell for itself which words interact meaningfully with which other words, without the need for an outside agent to put each word specifically into one category or another.

CHAPTER 6

Computer-Generated Text

AI researchers have made numerous attempts to produce programs which generate meaningful, coherent *text*—stories, reports, etc. This undertaking is a complex and difficult one, and their efforts, though interesting, have not met with much success. One program of this type is Sheldon Klein's "novel writer," which writes 2000-word mystery stories. The following sentences are the first few lines of one of the program's stories, as quoted by Margaret Boden:

> The day was Monday. The pleasant weather was sunny. Lady Buxley was in a park. James ran into Lady Buxley. James talked with Lady Buxley. Lady Buxley flirted with James. James invited Lady Buxley. James liked Lady Buxley. Lady Buxley liked James. Lady Buxley was with James in a hotel. Lady Buxley was near James. James caressed Lady Buxley with passion. James was Lady Buxley's lover. Marion following them saw the affair. Marion was jealous.

In spite of the difficulties it might prove an interesting task to attempt a story-generating program something like Klein's. It would produce different types of stories, depending on the contents of its vocabulary. Its operation would be similar to the HAIKU program in that it would generate sentences based on certain built-in, predefined patterns. However, more room would have to be allowed for variation in the individual sentences, or the output would quickly become monotonous.

If a program were written according to these specifications, what we would wind up with is not a story writer, but a sentence writer. But if the words of the vocabulary were chosen with care, the resulting sentences would seem to hang together and the result would be, hopefully, a story of sorts. Once again, the program used to generate the story would be built around a random-number generator.

The Building Blocks of a Sentence

What is the best way to build a sentence? To find the answer to this question let's analyze a typical sentence into its constituent parts so we'll know just what we have to work with.

Our typical sentence would very likely consist of a *noun phrase* followed by a *verb phrase*. In symbolic form the components could be represented like this:

S: NP   VP

But this immediately raises a question as to the composition of noun phrases and verb phrases. A typical noun phrase might consist of an article, followed by no, one, or two adjectives, followed by a noun:

NP: ART   ADJ(s)*   NOUN

where the asterisk is taken to mean that the indicated item is optional.

A noun phrase could also consist of a name or *proper noun,* like this:

NP: PNOUN

Notice that ART, ADJ, NOUN, and PNOUN cannot be analyzed any further, since they refer to single items. These four parts of speech are four of the primitives which we will later use to build sentences.

A verb phrase might consist of a verb, followed by no or one adverb, followed by zero, one, two, or more prepositional phrases:

VP: VERB   AVERB*   PP(s)*

VERB and AVERB are primitives, but PP can be analyzed into the form

PP: PREP   NP

This gives us seven primitives, ART, ADJ, NOUN, PNOUN, VERB, AVERB, and PREP, which can be used to build sentences; we also have the syntactic patterns which allow us to arrange these primitives grammatically. For instance, to construct a grammatical

PP, we must first get a PREP and then an NP; the NP in turn requires that we get an article, possibly one or two adjectives, and a noun, in that order. This process of constructing a PP is illustrated in Fig. 6-1.

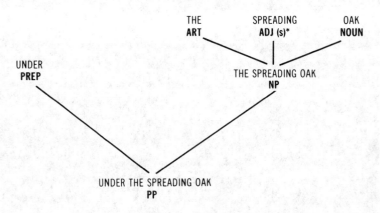

Fig. 6-1. Building a prepositional phrase.

Please note that we are limited to only a very small subset of the set of possible English sentences when we employ only these few parts of speech and syntactic patterns. Our aim is not the very ambitious one of writing a program which is capable of generating *any* grammatical sentence, but rather that of writing a program which is capable of generating *some* grammatical sentences.

Notice also that we will inevitably run into the same problem that we encountered in the HAIKU program, the problem of semantics. Under the scheme just described a PP like "behind the orange swirling sound" can be generated. This PP conforms to the syntactic rules of the English language and thus is perfectly grammatical; it is also perfect nonsense.

AUTOWRITER

Now let's look at a program, AUTOWRITER, which generates sentences according to the scheme just described. See the display in Fig. 6-2.

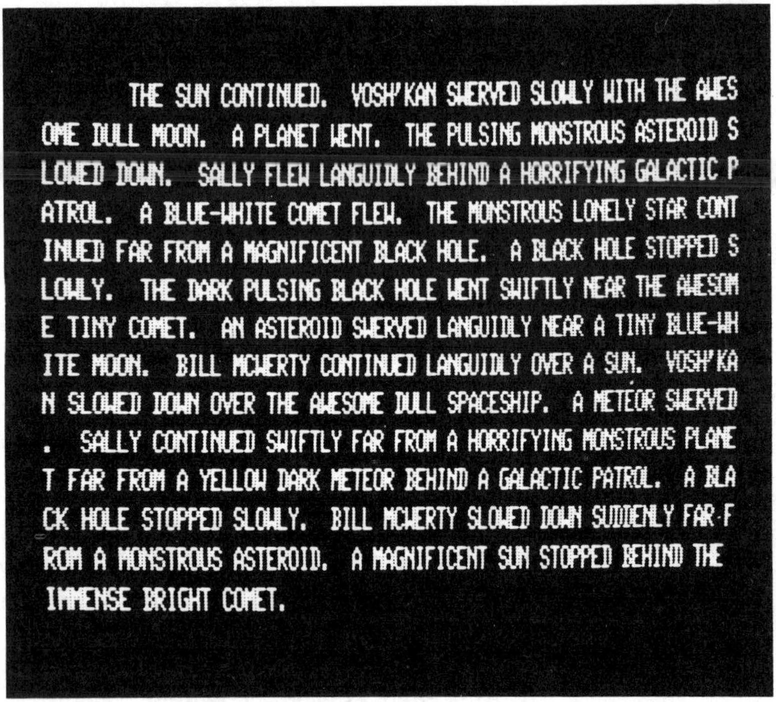

THE SUN CONTINUED. VOSH'KAN SWERVED SLOWLY WITH THE AWES
OME DULL MOON. A PLANET WENT. THE PULSING MONSTROUS ASTEROID S
LOWED DOWN. SALLY FLEW LANGUIDLY BEHIND A HORRIFYING GALACTIC P
ATROL. A BLUE-WHITE COMET FLEW. THE MONSTROUS LONELY STAR CONT
INUED FAR FROM A MAGNIFICENT BLACK HOLE. A BLACK HOLE STOPPED S
LOWLY. THE DARK PULSING BLACK HOLE WENT SWIFTLY NEAR THE AWESOM
E TINY COMET. AN ASTEROID SWERVED LANGUIDLY NEAR A TINY BLUE-WH
ITE MOON. BILL MCWERTY CONTINUED LANGUIDLY OVER A SUN. VOSH'KA
N SLOWED DOWN OVER THE AWESOME DULL SPACESHIP. A METEOR SWERVED
. SALLY CONTINUED SWIFTLY FAR FROM A HORRIFYING MONSTROUS PLANE
T FAR FROM A YELLOW DARK METEOR BEHIND A GALACTIC PATROL. A BLA
CK HOLE STOPPED SLOWLY. BILL MCWERTY SLOWED DOWN SUDDENLY FAR F
ROM A MONSTROUS ASTEROID. A MAGNIFICENT SUN STOPPED BEHIND THE
IMMENSE BRIGHT COMET.

Fig. 6-2. Video display of computer running AUTOWRITER.

Supervisor

Here is the AUTOWRITER supervisor:

```
10 '           Supervisor
20 GOSUB 230       ' Initialization
30 GOSUB 430       ' Sentence with or without proper noun?
40 IF RAN > 1 THEN 50 ELSE 90
50 GOSUB 460       ' Get article
60 GOSUB 490       ' Get adjective(s), if any
70 GOSUB 570       ' Get noun
80 GOTO 100
90 GOSUB 600       ' Get proper noun
100 GOSUB 630      ' Get verb
110 GOSUB 660      ' Get adverb, if any
120 GOSUB 700      ' Prepositional phrase?
130 IF RAN > 1 THEN 140 ELSE 200
140 GOSUB 730      ' Get preposition
150 GOSUB 460
160 GOSUB 490
170 GOSUB 570
180 GOSUB 760      ' Another prepositional phrase?
190 IF RAN > 1 THEN 140 ELSE 200
200 GOSUB 790      ' Check articles
210 GOSUB 870      ' Add punctuation to sentence and print
220 GOTO 30
```

An important point needs to be made about the structure of the supervisor. AUTOWRITER contains thirteen subroutines. All thirteen of these subroutines are controlled from the program's top level, i.e., from within the supervisor routine. The program was written this way not because it was convenient; it would be easier and more logical to structure the supervisor so that it calls only a couple of subroutines, for instance an NP-generating subroutine and a VP-generating subroutine. The NP- and VP-generating subroutines would then, independently of the supervisor, call the subroutines which they need to construct an NP or VP. For instance, the NP-generating subroutine would call the ART-generating subroutine, optionally the ADJ-generating subroutine, and finally the NOUN-generating subroutine. AUTOWRITER employs a different control structure in order to make the flow of control easier to trace.

The supervisor operates fairly straightforwardly. After the initialization routine at 230, one subroutine after another is called, depending on the part of speech that is needed. Sometimes a "decision-making" subroutine is called, such as the ones at 430 and 760, which decides (via a random number) whether a noun phrase should contain a common or proper noun, or whether another prepositional phrase should be added to the sentence. The operation of the supervisor after initialization can be summarized as follows:

(1) Determine whether or not the sentence should contain a PNOUN.
(2) If the sentence will *not* contain a PNOUN, generate an ART, generate 0, 1, or 2 ADJ(s), generate a NOUN. Go to (4).
(3) If the sentence *will* contain a PNOUN, generate the PNOUN. Go to (4).
(4) Generate a VERB. Generate 0 or 1 AVERB.
(5) Determine whether or not the sentence should contain a PP.
(6) If the sentence will *not* contain a PP, go to (8).
(7) If the sentence *will* contain a PP, generate a PREP, generate an ART, generate 0, 1, or 2 ADJ(s), generate a NOUN. Determine whether another PP should be added to the sentence. If so, go to (7). If not, go to (8).
(8) Check ART(s) of sentence for agreement. Add period to end of sentence and print. Go to (1).

The initialization subroutine at line 230 stores the program vocabulary in seven arrays; this was the alternative data storage method discussed in connection with HAIKU which allows for more efficient data retrieval. The article-checking subroutine at 790, which makes sure that every article in the sentence agrees with the word it precedes, is exactly the same routine as the one in HAIKU.

Getting a Component

Most of the subroutines called by the supervisor have the task of obtaining one or more components needed for the construction of a sentence. Here is one of those subroutines:

```
490 '          Get adjective(s), if any
500 RAN = RND(3)
510 IF RAN > 1 THEN 520 ELSE 560
520 SENT$ = SENT$ + " " + AD$(RND(ADJNMB))
530 IF Z = 1 THEN 550
540 RAN = RND(2): IF RAN = 1 THEN Z = 1: GOSUB 520
550 Z = 0
560 RETURN
```

The subroutine gets zero, one, or two adjectives to modify the noun in an NP. This, of course, allows greater variation in the individual sentences, since the resulting NP may contain one adjective, or two, or it may contain no adjectives at all.

Line 500 gets a random integer between 1 and 3 and assigns this value to RAN. If RAN > 1 control passes to line 520, but if RAN = 1 control returns to the supervisor and no adjective is generated. Thus about one-third of the NPs generated by the program will contain no modifiers. Line 520 gets the adjective from the vocabulary and puts it (along with a blank to separate words) into string variable SENT$. The adjective is obtained from the vocabulary by generating a random number between 1 and ADJNMB; ADJNMB is the number of adjectives contained in the vocabulary and is set by line 290 of the initialization routine. This random number value is then used to specify an element in array AD$, which holds all of the program's adjectives (cf. line 380). For example, if the random number is 8, the adjective that is incorporated into the sentence will be the adjective stored in AD$(8), the eighth adjective in the vocabulary.

Line 540 determines if a second modifier should be incorporated. About 50 percent of the NPs which have adjectives will contain the second adjective. The subroutine gets this second adjective by calling itself (or rather a portion of itself, beginning with line 520). Variable Z is used as a flag to ensure that the adjective-generation process is limited to a maximum of two adjectives.

Program Vocabulary

The sample vocabulary included with AUTOWRITER is a modest one, consisting of 55 items:

```
920 '           Vocabulary
930 '           A. Articles
940 DATA A, AN, THE
950 '           B. Nouns
960 DATA BLACK HOLE, SPACESHIP, STAR, PLANET, MOON, SUN
970 DATA COMET, GALACTIC FEDERATION, GALAXY, ASTEROID, METEOR
980 DATA ALIEN INVADER, GALACTIC PATROL
990 '           C. Proper Nouns
1000 DATA THE GALACTIC OVERLORD, BILL MCWERTY, SALLY, VOSH'KAN
1010 '           D. Adjectives
1020 DATA DARK, BRIGHT, PULSING, LONELY, MAGNIFICENT, DULL
1030 DATA RED, BLUE-WHITE, YELLOW, TINY, ENORMOUS, MONSTROUS
1040 DATA HORRIFYING, DISGUSTING, IMMENSE, LOVELY, AWESOME
1050 '           E. Verbs
1060 DATA STOPPED, FLEW, WENT, CONTINUED, SWERVED, SLOWED DOWN
1070 '           F. Adverbs
1080 DATA SLOWLY, LANGUIDLY, SWIFTLY, ERRATICALLY, SUDDENLY
1090 '           G. Prepositions
1100 DATA WITH, UNDER, BEHIND, OVER, NEAR, CLOSE TO, FAR FROM
```

This vocabulary was chosen, of course, with the aim of turning out old-fashioned science-fiction stories. The stories that are produced won't cause science-fiction writers any loss of sleep for fear of their jobs.

The vocabulary may be altered in any way the reader sees fit, as long as care is taken to make appropriate modifications to the initialization routines also. It would be interesting to try vocabularies that would cause the program to generate mysteries or Westerns. Some people, when confronted with a program of this type, like to fill the vocabulary with various off-color words, thus turning AUTOWRITER into a pornowriter.

AUTOWRITER Listing

Here is the program listing:

```
1 '           AUTOWRITER, Vers. 1.1
2 CLEAR 1000


10 '           Supervisor
20 GOSUB 230     ' Initialization
30 GOSUB 430     ' Sentence with or without proper noun?
40 IF RAN > 1 THEN 50 ELSE 90
50 GOSUB 460     ' Get article
60 GOSUB 490     ' Get adjective(s), if any
70 GOSUB 570     ' Get noun
80 GOTO 100
90 GOSUB 600     ' Get proper noun
100 GOSUB 630     ' Get verb
```

```
110 GOSUB 660      ' Get adverb, if any
120 GOSUB 700      ' Prepositional phrase?
130 IF RAN > 1 THEN 140 ELSE 200
140 GOSUB 730      ' Get preposition
150 GOSUB 460
160 GOSUB 490
170 GOSUB 570
180 GOSUB 760      ' Another prepositional phrase?
190 IF RAN > 1 THEN 140 ELSE 200
200 GOSUB 790      ' Check articles
210 GOSUB 870      ' Add punctuation to sentence and print
220 GOTO 30


230 '           Initialization
240 CLS: RANDOM
250 PRINT: PRINT "       ";
260 ARTNMB = 3
270 NOUNNMB = 13
280 PNOUNNMB = 4
290 ADJNMB = 17
300 VERBNMB = 6
310 AVNMB = 5
320 PREPNMB = 7
330 DIM NO$(13)
340 DIM AD$(17)
350 FOR I = 1 TO ARTNMB: READ AR$(I): NEXT I
360 FOR I = 1 TO NOUNNMB: READ NO$(I): NEXT I
370 FOR I = 1 TO PNOUNNMB: READ PN$(I): NEXT I
380 FOR I = 1 TO ADJNMB: READ AD$(I): NEXT I
390 FOR I = 1 TO VERBNMB: READ VE$(I): NEXT I
400 FOR I = 1 TO AVNMB: READ AV$(I): NEXT I
410 FOR I = 1 TO PREPNMB: READ PR$(I): NEXT I
420 RETURN


430 '           Sentence with or without proper noun?
440 RAN = RND(3)
450 RETURN


460 '           Get article
470 SENT$ = SENT$ + " " + AR$(RND(ARTNMB))
480 RETURN


490 '           Get adjective(s), if any
500 RAN = RND(3)
510 IF RAN > 1 THEN 520 ELSE 560
520 SENT$ = SENT$ + " " + AD$(RND(ADJNMB))
530 IF Z = 1 THEN 550
540 RAN = RND(2): IF RAN = 1 THEN Z = 1: GOSUB 520
550 Z = 0
560 RETURN


570 '           Get noun
580 SENT$ = SENT$ + " " + NO$(RND(NOUNNMB))
590 RETURN
```

```
600 '            Get proper noun
610 SENT$ = SENT$ + " " + PN$(RND(PNOUNNMB))
620 RETURN


630 '            Get verb
640 SENT$ = SENT$ + " " + VE$(RND(VERBNMB))
650 RETURN


660 '            Get adverb, if any
670 RAN = RND(3): IF RAN > 1 THEN 680 ELSE 690
680 SENT$ = SENT$ + " " + AV$(RND(AVNMB))
690 RETURN


700 '            Prepositional phrase?
710 RAN = RND(3)
720 RETURN


730 '            Get preposition
740 SENT$ = SENT$ + " " + PR$(RND(PREPNMB))
750 RETURN


760 '            Another prepositional phrase?
770 RAN = RND(2)
780 RETURN


790 '            Check articles
800 FOR I = 1 TO LEN(SENT$) - 2
810 IF MID$(SENT$, I, 3) = " A " THEN B$ =
    MID$(SENT$, I + 3, 1): IF B$ = "A" OR B$ = "E" OR B$ =
    "I" OR B$ = "O" OR B$ = "U" THEN SENT$ =
    LEFT$(SENT$, I + 1) + "N" + MID$(SENT$, I + 2)
820 NEXT I
830 FOR I = 1 TO LEN(SENT$) - 2
840 IF MID$(SENT$, I, 4) = " AN " THEN B$ =
    MID$(SENT$, I + 4, 1): IF B$ = "A" OR B$ = "E" OR B$ = "I"
    OR B$ = "O" OR B$ = "U" THEN 850 ELSE SENT$ =
    LEFT$(SENT$, I + 1) + MID$(SENT$, I + 3)
850 NEXT I
860 RETURN


870 '            Add punctuation to sentence and print
880 SENT$ = SENT$ + ". "
890 PRINT SENT$;
900 SENT$ = ""
910 RETURN


920 '            Vocabulary
930 '            A. Articles
940 DATA A, AN, THE
950 '            B. Nouns
960 DATA BLACK HOLE, SPACESHIP, STAR, PLANET, MOON, SUN
```

```
970 DATA COMET, GALACTIC FEDERATION, GALAXY, ASTEROID, METEOR
980 DATA ALIEN INVADER, GALACTIC PATROL
990 '          C. Proper Nouns
1000 DATA THE GALACTIC OVERLORD, BILL MCWERTY, SALLY, VOSH'KAN
1010 '          D. Adjectives
1020 DATA DARK, BRIGHT, PULSING, LONELY, MAGNIFICENT, DULL
1030 DATA RED, BLUE-WHITE, YELLOW, TINY, ENORMOUS, MONSTROUS
1040 DATA HORRIFYING, DISGUSTING, IMMENSE, LOVELY, AWESOME
1050 '          E. Verbs
1060 DATA STOPPED, FLEW, WENT, CONTINUED, SWERVED, SLOWED DOWN
1070 '          F. Adverbs
1080 DATA SLOWLY, LANGUIDLY, SWIFTLY, ERRATICALLY, SUDDENLY
1090 '          G. Prepositions
1100 DATA WITH, UNDER, BEHIND, OVER, NEAR, CLOSE TO, FAR FROM
```

Possible Modifications

(1) Many of the suggestions for changes to HAIKU can be applied equally well to AUTOWRITER. The program can be altered so that a given word is never incorporated twice into the same sentence, eliminating clumsy and inappropriate phrases like "MAGNIFICENT MAGNIFICENT GALAXY." Also, it is possible to categorize the vocabulary so that certain words are matched only with certain other words. To take an example, the present vocabulary contains only a few verbs, all of them having to do with motion, since these verbs must be used both for common and proper nouns, and motion verbs agree fairly well with both classes of nouns. But if the verbs in the vocabulary were divided into two sets, one set being applied exclusively to common nouns and the other exclusively to proper nouns, many more verbs could be incorporated into the program and the resulting output would be more varied and interesting.

(2) If your BASIC contains the POS function (see the Appendix for an explanation of POS) or its equivalent, the output of AUTOWRITER can be made to look much less crude when it is printed on the display. Subroutine 870 should be modified so that SENT$ is printed word by word. As SENT$ is printed, POS should be used to continuously check the current cursor position. When the current cursor position is within about ten spaces of the end of the horizontal display line, the routine should start looking for the next blank in SENT$ (signifying a space between two words). When it finds the next blank, it first prints a line feed/carriage return and then the rest of SENT$. This is a simple routine to work up and it virtually eliminates the division of a word between two lines on the display.

(3) A student might care to restructure the supervisor in such a way that AUTOWRITER generates grammatical sentences with a new and more useful syntax than the one supplied. For instance, the existing subroutine calls of the supervisor could be juggled

around and new calls to various subroutines could be inserted into the supervisor where needed, so that instead of stories AUTOWRITER would produce phony book reviews, reports, lab write-ups, and similar material. A new vocabulary appropriate to the task in mind would of course have to be selected. If anyone should try this, the author hereby disclaims all responsibility if the output is actually handed in to an instructor!

CHAPTER 7

Natural-Language Processing

In 1966 MIT computer scientist Joseph Weizenbaum put the finishing touches on a program which he called ELIZA, after the character Eliza Doolittle in Shaw's *Pygmalion*. ELIZA allowed the user to type a sentence at the keyboard—any sentence, no restriction on content or grammar—and the computer would respond with a sentence of its own. This response would usually be both appropriate and meaningful.

ELIZA was composed of two modules. One module contained the program's main routine; the other held what Weizenbaum referred to as a "script." A script was a set of rules which allowed ELIZA to carry on a conversation about a certain topic. Scripts were interchangeable, so that different scripts could be plugged into ELIZA to make it converse with the user on different subjects.

One script which Weizenbaum created for ELIZA caused the program to engage in a sort of mock psychiatric session in the manner of psychotherapist Carl R. Rogers. Rogers believed that psychotherapy was most effective when it was "nondirective," that is, the patient, when speaking with his or her psychotherapist, should be the one to lead the therapeutic process; the psychotherapist should refrain from attempting any formal guidance. During a therapeutic session, this would naturally tend to minimize the part of the psychotherapist while maximizing that of the patient. Weizenbaum realized that "nondirective" psychotherapy would be ideal for computer simulation, with the computer taking the part of the therapist.

The version of ELIZA which contained the psychotherapist script was known as DOCTOR. DOCTOR soon became perhaps the most famous computer program in the world, and justly so.

It produces spectacular results, even though it is by no means a complicated program, and it is fiendishly clever. Here is a sample of the kind of conversation one might have with a typical implementation of DOCTOR (computer's replies are all capitals):

I don't get along with my brother Bill.
TELL ME MORE ABOUT YOUR FAMILY.
There's five of us altogether. Bill is older.
PLEASE GO ON.
Even as a kid Bill always ignored my rights.
YOUR RIGHTS.
Yes. He never gave me a break.
YOU SEEM QUITE POSITIVE.

Though this exchange seems quite amazing at first glance, it is all accomplished through semantic trickery rather than by any real understanding on the part of DOCTOR of what is being said. At the risk of diminishing the program's impact by explaining how the rabbit is produced from the hat, let's discuss, in general terms, how DOCTOR manages to come up with sensible-sounding replies to statements like the ones above. We will be more specific about its operation later on when we construct a DOCTOR program of our own.

How DOCTOR Generates Its Replies

When a sentence is input to DOCTOR the program scans through it, looking for *keywords* (or *key phrases*). If a keyword is found, DOCTOR generates an automatic response; the content of the response is determined by the keyword. If no keyword is found, DOCTOR generates a "noncommittal" response. This, in a nutshell, is how the program operates.

The sentence "I don't get along with my brother Bill" contains the key phrase "my brother." Whenever the program encounters this phrase (or the related key phrases "my sister," "my mother," "my father," "my wife," "my husband," and "my children") it looks up the associated response in a table. This response happens to be "TELL ME MORE ABOUT YOUR FAMILY."

However, in "There's five of us altogether. Bill is older" no keywords are present. In this case the computer simply prints any one of several noncommittal replies, such as "PLEASE GO ON" or "I'M NOT SURE I UNDERSTAND YOU FULLY." These noncommittal responses will be more or less appropriate under most circumstances.

The keyword in "Even as a kid Bill always ignored my rights" is "my." Here the program picks up the phrase which begins with "my" and ends with the end of the sentence, changes the "my" to "Your," and prints the resultant phrase as its reply. The reply in this instance would be "YOUR RIGHTS." This, of course, is in imitation of human dialogue. Thus if the user had typed "My athlete's foot is acting up again" the program would solemnly repeat "YOUR ATHLETE'S FOOT IS ACTING UP AGAIN." DOCTOR did not reply "YOUR BROTHER BILL" to "I don't get along with my brother Bill" because "my brother" has a higher precedence than plain "my."

"Yes" is the keyword in "Yes. He never gave me a break," which prompts the automatic reply, "YOU SEEM QUITE POSITIVE."

DOCTOR contains other embellishments. One of the most ingenious of them involves the keyword "my." Whenever the person at the keyboard uses this word in a sentence, DOCTOR takes the phrase that begins with the first character after the "my" and ends with the end of the sentence. The resulting phrase is stored. From then on, when the user types in a sentence which contains no keywords, DOCTOR has a choice of options. Sometimes it will respond with one of the "noncommittal" replies such as "PLEASE GO ON." But on occasion it will do something entirely different: it will print the words "EARLIER YOU SAID THAT YOUR" (or perhaps "DOES THAT HAVE ANYTHING TO DO WITH THE FACT THAT YOUR") *plus* the phrase that was stored earlier. So if this stored phrase were "LIFE IS A SHAMBLES" (originally derived from, say, "Sometimes I think my life is a shambles") the phrase that would be printed as DOCTOR's reply would be "EARLIER YOU SAID THAT YOUR LIFE IS A SHAMBLES." (or, alternatively, "DOES THAT HAVE ANYTHING TO DO WITH THE FACT THAT YOUR LIFE IS A SHAMBLES?") which would have a good chance of being meaningful no matter what the user's previous sentence had been.

These are examples of the program at its best. Unfortunately, as we have stated, DOCTOR has no real understanding of the conversation in which it is engaged. Sometimes one of the gimmicks contained in the program will be applied to an improper situation, because DOCTOR can't begin to understand that the gimmick is not suitable for that situation. The resulting reply may be simply inappropriate, or it may be downright ridiculous.

For instance, if the user types "I'm surprised to be talking to a computer," the program keys on the word "computer" and prints the appropriate response "DO COMPUTERS WORRY YOU?" But if the user types "I'm a computer programmer by profession," DOCTOR is nevertheless still triggered by the keyword "computer" and prints the same response, which this time is inappropriate.

A further example: if the preceding sentence which contained "my" had been "My athlete's foot is acting up again" (instead of "Sometimes I think my life is a shambles") the program might later respond to a sentence that contains no keywords with "DOES THAT HAVE ANYTHING TO DO WITH THE FACT THAT YOUR ATHLETE'S FOOT IS ACTING UP AGAIN?" This would have to be termed ridiculous. And if the sentence had been "I don't get along with my girlfriend's brother" sooner or later DOCTOR would come up with "DOES THAT HAVE ANYTHING TO DO WITH THE FACT THAT YOUR GIRLFRIEND'S BROTHER?", which is gibberish.

Controversy Over DOCTOR

This resourceful program, as we have noted, quickly became very famous. Its creator, Joseph Weizenbaum, however, was displeased with the way DOCTOR came to be interpreted. In fact, his observations of how people reacted to the program led him to become a critic and even to some degree an opponent of artificial intelligence.

In his book *Computer Power and Human Reason* (1976) Weizenbaum explains what disturbed him about the reaction to DOCTOR. He found it amazing that many people, after a short period of interaction with DOCTOR, began to relate to the program intimate thoughts and feelings, just as if they were carrying on a serious conversation with a human psychiatrist. Weizenbaum referred to this understanding of the relationship as "powerful delusional thinking."

Another incident that he found upsetting was the proposal of Kenneth M. Colby, Professor of Psychiatry at UCLA and a practicing psychotherapist for many years, in regard to DOCTOR. Colby and two colleagues suggested that an expanded, improved version of DOCTOR be made available to mental hospitals and other mental institutions which were short of staff. DOCTOR, they said, could be implemented on a time-sharing computer system in each of these institutions, making it possible to handle hundreds of patients hourly. Weizenbaum wrote:

> I had thought it essential, as a prerequisite to the very possibility that one person might help another learn to cope with his emotional problems, that the helper himself participate in the other's experience of those problems and, in large part by way of his own empathic recognition of them, himself come to understand them. . . . That it was possible for even one practicing psychiatrist to advocate that this crucial com-

ponent of the therapeutic process be entirely supplanted by pure technique—*that* I had not imagined!

Colby replied:

That the function of psychotherapy is to dispense respect, understanding, and love is one of those characterizations from the layman which takes clinicians aback. It seems to confuse psychotherapy with, for example, marriage. To confound professional working relationships with affectionate marriage relationships reveals a fundamental misunderstanding of what psychotherapy is all about . . . . There are great difficulties in programming a computer system to participate in therapeutic dialogs. But even if it could be achieved and even if it helped people, it ought not to be done at all, according to our critic. Why not? He offers no reasons: he seems confident that his word is enough. Presumably he believes it is better to let people suffer than have them helped by a computer.*

Whatever one's feelings may be in regards to the advisability of using DOCTOR on psychiatric patients, it is hard to deny the fascination and effectiveness of the program. In particular, as Weizenbaum himself notes, DOCTOR makes a striking demonstration program to show to people who have not been previously acquainted with computers or programming.

The Artificial Paranoid

Meanwhile, Kenneth Colby, his interest in computer modelling of human behavior presumably sparked by the Weizenbaum program, went on to write a program of his own, one which was in some ways even more original than DOCTOR. This program was PARRY. It provides an interesting complement to DOCTOR, since while DOCTOR plays the role of a psychiatrist, PARRY plays the role of the patient on the psychiatrist's couch!

PARRY, in short, simulates the responses of a young man suffering from paranoid schizophrenia. PARRY is an interactive program like DOCTOR. A person at the computer keyboard types in queries or comments; responses are printed by the program. That it is a good simulation is attested to by the fact that when Colby sent a transcript of one of PARRY's conversations to psychiatrists around the country, along with a transcript of an actual interview with a paranoid patient, and asked the psychiatrists to determine,

---

*Quoted in *Machines Who Think,* by Pamela McCorduck (W. H. Freeman & Co., 1979).

if they could, which was real and which was the ringer, only 51 percent of the psychiatrists managed to pick the right transcript. Of course, 51 percent is no better than if they had chosen at random.

PARRY has two modes in which it operates. In its "weak" mode, it displays fewer symptoms of paranoia than when it is in its "strong" mode. Here is an extract from a conversation with PARRY in its "weak" mode:

How long have you been in the hospital?
ABOUT A WEEK.
Are you depressed?
NO.
Were you taking drugs?
NO.
What is your problem?
PEOPLE MAKE ME NERVOUS.
How do they do that?
THEY STARE AT ME.
Why?
MAYBE THEY DON'T LIKE THE WAY I LOOK OR SOMETHING.
Do you look unusual in some way?
WHY ARE YOU INTERESTED IN MY LOOKS?
Because you said people stare at you.
WELL, SOMETIMES.
How do you get along with people?
I DON'T COMMUNICATE VERY MUCH WITH THE OTHERS.
Why not?
THEY DON'T REALIZE WHAT'S GOING ON MOST OF THE TIME.

Here is the same program operating in the "strong" mode:

Why are you in the hospital?
I SHOULDN'T BE HERE.
Who brought you here?
THE POLICE.
What trouble did you have with the police?
COPS DON'T DO THEIR JOB.
What do they do instead?
COPS ARREST THE WRONG PEOPLE.
They arrest the right ones sometimes.
THE LAW SHOULD GET THOSE ITALIAN CROOKS.
Are you Italian?
MY BACKGROUND IS BRITISH BUT I WAS BORN IN THIS COUNTRY.
Do you know any Italian crooks?
I TRY TO AVOID THE UNDERWORLD.
Are you afraid of the underworld?
THE MAFIA ARE THE WORST GANGSTERS.
Are you connected with the mafia?
YOU KNOW, THEY KNOW ME.
How do they know you?
THEY SPY ON ME.
Why do they?

THEY WANT TO GET FALSE EVIDENCE TO FRAME ME.
What do they have against you?
THEY ARE OUT TO GET ME.
What for?
I HAVE INCRIMINATING EVIDENCE AGAINST THE MAFIA.

The internal mechanisms of PARRY, like DOCTOR, are completely grounded in semantic trickery. PARRY only *seems* to understand the questions of the interviewer; actually it has no understanding of the conversation whatsoever. When asked a question with which it is not sophisticated enough to deal, PARRY will respond with an inappropriate answer, just as DOCTOR would. PARRY, however, has an advantage over DOCTOR in that we have a tendency to expect inappropriate answers from a person who is mentally ill; our expectations when we deal with a presumably competent psychiatrist are rather different.

Understanding Natural Language

Research in artificial intelligence has progressed substantially since 1966–67, when DOCTOR and PARRY were written, and researchers have since developed programs which do indeed understand natural languages such as English to some extent, instead of merely pretending to understand them.

But what exactly do we mean when we say a program "understands" natural language? Natural-language researcher Wendy G. Lehnert provides an answer. Says Lehnert:

When people understand stories, they can demonstrate their understanding by answering questions about the story. Because questions can be devised to query any aspect of text comprehension, the ability to answer questions is the strongest possible demonstration of understanding. . . . If a computer is said to understand a story, we must demand of the computer the same demonstrations of understanding that we require of people. Until such demands are met, we have no way of evaluating text-understanding programs. Any computer programmer can write a program that inputs text. If the programmer assures us that the program "understands" text, it is a bit like being reassured by a used car dealer about a suspiciously low speedometer reading. Only when we can ask a program to answer questions about what it reads will we be in a position to assess that program's comprehension.

Consider the following BASIC program:

```
10 INPUT A$
20 PRINT "I UNDERSTAND."
30 GOTO 10
```

A conversation with this program might go like this:

```
? I TOOK THE DOG FOR A WALK THIS MORNING.
I UNDERSTAND.
? IT WAS RAINING SO I BROUGHT MY UMBRELLA.
I UNDERSTAND.
```

This is truly an absurd program because even though it keeps assuring the person at the other end that it "understands," it of course does not understand so much as one word of the conversation. Following Wendy Lehnert's line of thought, we can demonstrate the program's lack of understanding by asking questions about the text it has input:

```
? WHAT DID I DO THIS MORNING?
I UNDERSTAND.
? WHAT WAS THE WEATHER LIKE.
I UNDERSTAND.
```

These inappropriate answers clearly reveal the program for what it is: a faker. DOCTOR and PARRY are not nearly so crude, but, as was emphasized, their understanding of the conversations in which they engage is likewise zero. This could be shown by putting questions to them like the preceding ones.

On the other hand, suppose we had a program that gave these replies to our questions:

```
? WHAT DID I DO THIS MORNING?
YOU TOOK THE DOG FOR A WALK.
? WHAT WAS THE WEATHER LIKE?
IT WAS RAINING.
```

In this case, since the program can correctly answer questions relating to material that was previously input, we can fairly say that it has "understood" the conversation.

In recent years a number of programs have been developed which exhibit understanding of this sort. They are able to engage in fairly natural-sounding dialogue. When asked questions about information that had been imparted during the course of the dialogue, they make appropriate responses. But they have one debilitating weakness in common: their "domain," the range of subjects on which they can intelligently converse, is quite limited.

These programs are referred to as Q/A (question-answering) programs. The first of them was Terry Winograd's SHRDLU, completed in 1971. SHRDLU's domain is restricted to the world of geometric figures. When the program is run, a number of different-colored blocks, pyramids, and boxes appear on the display. The user types in commands involving the movement of the object from one place on the screen to another. SHRDLU complies by moving the objects around on the screen as requested. The user can ask various questions about the new positionings; SHRDLU will respond correctly, as long as the questions are limited to the geometrical-objects domain. Here is a sample conversation with SHRDLU:

Pick up a big red block.
OK.
Find a block which is taller than the one you are holding and put it into the box.
OK.
What does the box contain?
THE BLUE PYRAMID AND THE BLUE BOX.
What is the pyramid supported by?
THE BOX.
Will you please stack up both of the red blocks and either a green cube or a pyramid.
OK.
Which cube is sitting on the table?
THE LARGE GREEN ONE WHICH SUPPORTS THE RED PYRAMID.
Is there a large block behind a pyramid?
YES, THREE OF THEM: A LARGE RED ONE, A LARGE GREEN CUBE, AND THE BLUE ONE.

This conversation is nothing short of astonishing. Nor, in this brief excerpt, have we fully demonstrated SHRDLU's abilities. SHRDLU is a landmark program in artificial intelligence research.

The Q/A programs which came after SHRDLU each occupied a domain unique to itself. Thus Woods's LSNLIS answers questions about the rock samples brought back from the moon by the Apollo 11 astronauts. Waltz's PLANES answers questions about aircraft maintenance and similar topics. A program with a less exotic data base is Scragg's LUIGI; LUIGI answers questions relating to meal preparation like "What utensils would I need if I toasted bread?" Bobrow's GUS plays the part of a travel agent, and advises the user as to flights, hotels, etc.

DOCTOR

The DOCTOR program which is developed below contains most of the features of the original. The program will initially ask the user or "patient" to "PLEASE STATE YOUR PROBLEM." The patient then types out a reply on the keyboard and presses the carriage return. DOCTOR will respond and the dialogue has begun.

Fig. 7-1 shows the video display of a computer running DOCTOR. Lines preceded by a question mark are user input; other lines are generated by the computer.

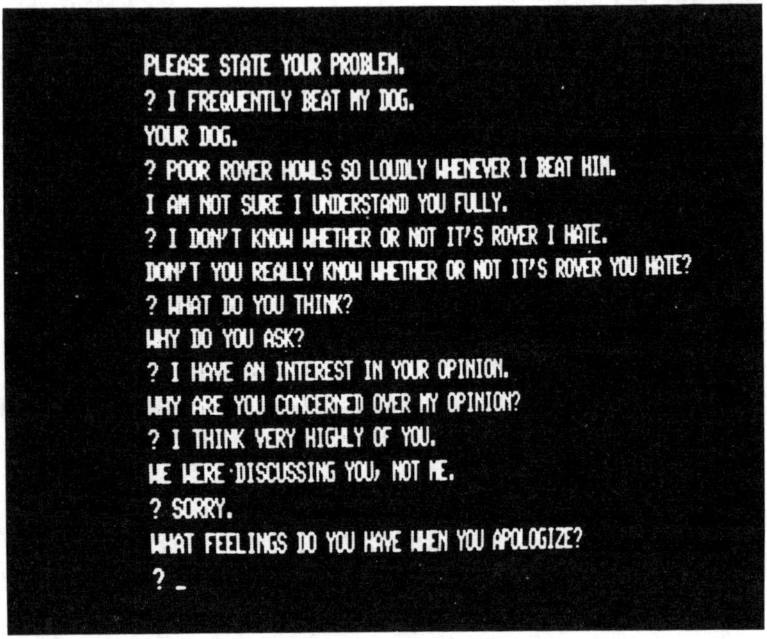

```
PLEASE STATE YOUR PROBLEM.
? I FREQUENTLY BEAT MY DOG.
YOUR DOG.
? POOR ROVER HOWLS SO LOUDLY WHENEVER I BEAT HIM.
I AM NOT SURE I UNDERSTAND YOU FULLY.
? I DON'T KNOW WHETHER OR NOT IT'S ROVER I HATE.
DON'T YOU REALLY KNOW WHETHER OR NOT IT'S ROVER YOU HATE?
? WHAT DO YOU THINK?
WHY DO YOU ASK?
? I HAVE AN INTEREST IN YOUR OPINION.
WHY ARE YOU CONCERNED OVER MY OPINION?
? I THINK VERY HIGHLY OF YOU.
WE WERE DISCUSSING YOU, NOT ME.
? SORRY.
WHAT FEELINGS DO YOU HAVE WHEN YOU APOLOGIZE?
? _
```

Fig. 7-1. Video display of a computer running DOCTOR.

Supervisor

Here is the DOCTOR supervisor:

```
10 '          Supervisor
20 GOSUB 90    ' Initialization
30 GOSUB 160   ' Input (and associated functions)
40 GOSUB 250   ' Swap word for opposite form
50 GOSUB 410   ' Keyword processing
60 GOSUB 910   ' Marker remover
70 GOSUB 970   ' Doctor's reply
80 GOTO 30
```

The supervisor is composed of six subroutines. (There are three further subroutines, all of them very brief, at the end of the program; they are never called by the supervisor, only by the six main routines.) Let's consider each of the six subroutines in turn.

Initialization

This routine is, as usual, called only once during the course of the program; it takes care of variable assignments and other necessary tasks:

```
90 '          Initialization
100 NM = 28
110 NU = 82
120 RANDOM
130 CLS: PRINT: PRINT
140 PRINT "PLEASE STATE YOUR PROBLEM."
150 RETURN
```

NM, NU, and all other variables used in the program are defined in Table 7-1. Variables which end in "$" contain strings while the others contain numbers.

Table 7-1. Variables Used by DOCTOR

Variable	Contains
DR$	DOCTOR's reply to the patient
JU	Number which tells ON. . .GOTO statement which line to jump to
KE$	Keyword (or key phrase)
NM	Number of data items in the word-swapping routine
NU	Number of data items in the keyword processing routine, i.e., number of keywords/key phrases
PA$	Patient's reply to DOCTOR
PR$	Patient's previous reply to DOCTOR
PS	Number which refers to a position in a string
RAN	Pseudorandom number
TE$	In the word-swapping routine a tense or form of a certain word as supplied by the patient
TN$	In the word-swapping routine a tense or form of a certain word which the program will substitute for the equivalent TE$
X	Number which serves as flag to allow program to skip routines when needful
YO$	Phrase which follows "MY" in PA$

Input

The input (and associated functions) routine gets a sentence from the patient:

```
160 '           Input (and associated functions)
170 RESTORE
180 X = 0: PA$ = ""
190 INPUT PA$
200 IF PA$ = "" THEN PRINT "DO YOU HAVE A PROBLEM?": X = 1:
    GOTO 240
210 IF PA$ = PR$ THEN PRINT "PLEASE DON'T REPEAT YOURSELF!":
    X = 1: GOTO 240
220 PR$ = PA$
230 PA$ = " " + LEFT$(PA$, LEN(PA$) - 1) + " "
240 RETURN
```

The patient's sentence is input into string variable PA$ in line 190. Since INPUT is used for this task, if the sentence contains commas, colons, or other termination characters (depending on the BASIC in use), only part of the sentence (up to the first termination character) will be input into PA$. In some BASICs this can be avoided by enclosing the sentence in quotation marks if it will contain one or more commas. Quotes are not necessary around sentences which don't contain commas or other termination characters. If your BASIC includes the LINE INPUT statement or its equivalent, you should use LINE INPUT PA$ in place of INPUT PA$; commas may then be input to the program with impunity.

If PA$ is the empty string, i.e., the patient simply hit the carriage return without bothering to type anything, line 200 has a special message for him or her. PR$ contains the patient's previous response to DOCTOR. If the present response, contained in PA$, is the same as the response in PR$, line 210 has another special message for the patient. Notice that when DOCTOR's response is printed right away, as in lines 200 and 210, flag variable X is set to 1. This allows the program to skip over routines that it won't need, such as the keyword processing routine, and get back to the input routine, ready to accept another sentence from the patient. Line 230 prepares PA$ for processing by removing the punctuation from the end of PA$ and placing a blank at the beginning and another at the end.

Swap Word for Opposite Form

Here is the word-swapping routine:

```
250 '            Swap word for opposite form
260 IF X = 1 THEN 400
270 FOR I = 1 TO NM/2
280 READ TE$, TN$
290 FOR PS = 1 TO LEN(PA$) - LEN(TE$) + 1
300 IF TE$ = MID$(PA$, PS, LEN(TE$)) THEN PA$ =
    LEFT$(PA$, PS - 1) + TN$ + MID$(PA$, PS + LEN(TE$))
310 DATA " MOM "," MOTHER "," DAD "," FATHER "
320 DATA " DREAMS "," DREAM "
330 DATA " I "," YOU@ "," YOU "," I "," ME "," YOU "
340 DATA " MY "," YOUR* "
350 DATA " YOUR "," MY "," MYSELF "," YOURSELF* "
360 DATA " YOURSELF "," MYSELF "
370 DATA " I'M "," YOU'RE* "," YOU'RE "," I'M "," AM "," ARE@ "
380 DATA " WERE "," WAS "
390 NEXT PS, I
400 RETURN
```

This subroutine reads pairs of data items from lines 310–380; the first item is assigned to TE$, the second, to TN$. Then the subroutine scans through PA$, looking for TE$. If TE$ is present, it is removed and TN$ is put in its place.

What's the reason for this? It should be kept in mind that DOCTOR likes to use all or part of the patient's sentence (PA$) in its own reply. In order to be able to do this grammatically, the program has to be able to change the form or tense of certain verbs, pronouns, and other words so that its reply seems to be addressed to the patient. For example, suppose the patient's sentence is "MY BOSS IS DRIVING ME CRAZY." The program would like to repeat that sentence back to the patient as its reply. The word-swapping subroutine changes "MY" to "YOUR*" and "ME" to "YOU" so that the reply sentence (up to this point) reads "YOUR* BOSS IS DRIVING YOU CRAZY." (The asterisks and @ signs after certain words are markers to keep the program from getting confused between two uses of the same word later on in the program.)

"MOM" is always replaced by "MOTHER" and "DAD" by "FATHER" in DOCTOR's responses. This is done to put some variation in the replies as well as to give them added dignity as befits a learned psychotherapist.

Keyword Processing

The long subroutine which handles keyword processing is divided into two parts. Section A checks the patient's sentence for keywords. The present implementation of DOCTOR contains fully 82 keywords/key phrases; all 82 of them are stored as data in this section. After each keyword is a number. A keyword and its associated number are read into KE$ and JU. The program now scans through PA$, looking for the keyword. If it *doesn't* find the keyword, it reads a new keyword and its associated number into the two variables and commences the scanning operation once again. If it *does* find the keyword somewhere in the sentence, the portion of the sentence *following the keyword* is stored in DR$. Control then returns to the supervisor.

If the program goes all the way through the list of keywords without locating any of them in PA$, control falls through to section B of the routine:

```
790 '          B. No keywords found
800 IF YO$ = "" THEN 810 ELSE RAN = RND(5):
    ON RAN GOTO 810, 810, 810, 860, 860
810 RAN = RND(4): ON RAN GOTO 820, 830, 840, 850
820 PRINT "I AM NOT SURE I UNDERSTAND YOU FULLY.": X = 1:
    GOTO 900
830 PRINT "PLEASE GO ON.": X = 1: GOTO 900
840 PRINT "WHAT DOES THAT SUGGEST TO YOU?": X = 1: GOTO 900
850 PRINT "DO YOU FEEL STRONGLY ABOUT DISCUSSING SUCH THINGS?":
    X = 1: GOTO 900
860 RAN = RND(3): ON RAN GOTO 870, 880, 890
870 PRINT "LET'S DISCUSS FURTHER WHY YOUR" + YO$ + ".": X = 1:
    GOTO 900
880 PRINT "EARLIER YOU SAID YOUR" + YO$ + ".": X = 1: GOTO 900
890 PRINT
    "DOES THAT HAVE ANYTHING TO DO WITH THE FACT THAT YOUR" +
    YO$ + "?": X = 1: GOTO 900
900 RETURN
```

This section is primarily a collection of "noncommittal" responses, one of which the program is forced to choose, since it really has no clues that would enable it to deliver a more appropriate answer. Which of these replies will be chosen is determined by a random-number generator and the following algorithm:

(1) If YO$ contains something other than the empty string (e.g., YO$ = "LIFE IS A SHAMBLES"), then two-fifths of the time the answer generated will be something built around this phrase, such as "LET'S DISCUSS FURTHER WHY YOUR LIFE IS A SHAMBLES" or "EARLIER YOU SAID YOUR LIFE IS A SHAMBLES." Three-fifths of the time, however, a standard "noncommittal" reply will be generated, such as "PLEASE GO ON" or "WHAT DOES THAT SUGGEST TO YOU?"

(2) If the contents of YO$ is the empty string, indicating that the patient has not yet typed in a sentence containing a "my" phrase, then in all cases a standard "noncommittal" reply will be generated.

Marker Remover

This little subroutine simply extracts leftover asterisks and @ signs from DR$.

DOCTOR's Reply

This brings us to the central subroutine of the program, the one which contains the data and string manipulations necessary to generate the doctor's reply.

The subroutine has two sections, A and B. Here is section A:

```
970 '          Doctor's reply
980 '          A. Line to jump to
990 IF X = 1 THEN 1470
1000 ON JU GOTO 1020,1030,1040,1050,1060,1070,1080,1090,1100,
1110,1120,1130,1140,1150,1160,1170,1180,1190,1200,1210,1220,
1230,1240,1250,1260,1270,1290,1290,1300,1310,1320,1370,1380,
1390,1400,1410,1420,1430,1440,1450,1460
```

You will recall the numbers stored after the keywords in the keyword-processing subroutine; here's where they come in. When the keyword-processing routine locates a keyword, the associated number is assigned to JU. Now, in line 1000 of the doctor's reply routine, JU still contains that number. Suppose the number is 10. The ON JU GOTO statement will count over to the tenth line number following the GOTO, and program control will be transferred to that line (1110). Line 1110 contains a short routine to supply the doctor's response to the patient. This response will sound like an appropriate reply, since it was designed to match the keyword which the program located in the patient's sentence.

Response Generation Example

Let's look at an example of how DOCTOR produces a response to an input sentence; we will trace the response from the beginning of the program to the end. Let's suppose the patient, having heard certain nasty rumors about his computer shrink, suddenly, during a session with the computer, demands,

WERE YOU OUT WITH MY WIFE LAST NIGHT?

The input subroutine inputs this sentence into PA$. The question mark is stripped off and blanks are put at the beginning and end of the sentence, so that PA$ = " WERE YOU OUT WITH MY WIFE LAST NIGHT ."

The word-swapping subroutine changes the forms of the verb and pronouns in PA$, so PA$ = " WAS I OUT WITH YOUR* WIFE LAST NIGHT ."

The keyword-processing subroutine scans PA$ for keywords/ key phrases. There are actually three, "WAS I," "YOUR*," and "YOUR* WIFE." However, "YOUR* WIFE" is precedent over "YOUR*" (by virtue of the fact that it comes before "YOUR*" in the data list) and "WAS I" is precedent over "YOUR* WIFE." Therefore, the key phrase is "WAS I," and the number assigned to JU is the number immediately following "WAS I," which is 12. Now line 470 takes the contents of PA$ and discards all of it up to and including the keyword/key phrase. The remainder is put into DR$, the doctor's reply, so that DR$ = " OUT WITH YOUR* WIFE LAST NIGHT."

The marker-removing subroutine deletes the asterisk in "YOUR*." DR$ = " OUT WITH YOUR WIFE LAST NIGHT."

Section A, line 1000, of the doctor's reply subroutine counts over to the twelfth line number (since JU = 12). The twelfth line number is 1130. Control is therefore transferred to line 1130 of section B. Line 1130 contains the instructions PRINT "WOULD YOU LIKE TO BELIEVE I WAS" + DR$ + "?". Since DR$ = " OUT WITH YOUR WIFE LAST NIGHT," the sentence that is printed is

WOULD YOU LIKE TO BELIEVE I WAS OUT WITH YOUR WIFE LAST NIGHT?

Control now returns to the supervisor, which calls up the input subroutine once more to receive the patient's next sentence— doubtless an interesting one.

Time Considerations

DOCTOR must do a great deal of sifting through the input sentence, searching for keywords as well as for pronouns and other words which must be swapped. Due to the amount of time consumed by the searching process, the program runs rather slowly.

How much time the program will need to formulate a reply depends on several factors, primarily (a) the speed of the BASIC in which the program is written and (b) the length of the sentence to which the program is responding. Obviously, a program written in a relatively slow BASIC will take much longer to respond to a long sentence than a program written in a fast BASIC that is responding to a shorter sentence. There is little you can do to improve the speed of your BASIC, but you can certainly limit your sentences to medium length, about 50 characters. DOCTOR should respond to a sentence of this length in about 30 to 60 seconds. All input sentences, incidentally, must end with a period, a question mark, an exclamation point, or some other form of punctuation.

DOCTOR Listing

Here is the program in its entirety:

```
1 '            DOCTOR, Vers. 2.1
2 CLEAR 1000

10 '            Supervisor
20 GOSUB 90       ' Initialization
30 GOSUB 160      ' Input (and associated functions)
40 GOSUB 250      ' Swap word for opposite form
50 GOSUB 410      ' Keyword processing
60 GOSUB 910      ' Marker remover
70 GOSUB 970      ' Doctor's reply
80 GOTO 30

90 '            Initialization
100 NM = 28
110 NU = 82
120 RANDOM
130 CLS: PRINT: PRINT
140 PRINT "PLEASE STATE YOUR PROBLEM."
150 RETURN

160 '            Input (and associated functions)
170 RESTORE
180 X = 0: PA$ = ""
190 INPUT PA$
200 IF PA$ = "" THEN PRINT "DO YOU HAVE A PROBLEM?": X = 1:
    GOTO 240
210 IF PA$ = PR$ THEN PRINT "PLEASE DON'T REPEAT YOURSELF!":
    X = 1: GOTO 240
220 PR$ = PA$
230 PA$ = " " + LEFT$(PA$, LEN(PA$) - 1) + " "
240 RETURN

250 '            Swap word for opposite form
260 IF X = 1 THEN 400
270 FOR I = 1 TO NM/2
280 READ TE$, TN$
290 FOR PS = 1 TO LEN(PA$) - LEN(TE$) + 1
300 IF TE$ = MID$(PA$, PS, LEN(TE$)) THEN PA$ =
    LEFT$(PA$, PS - 1) + TN$ + MID$(PA$, PS + LEN(TE$))
310 DATA " MOM "," MOTHER "," DAD "," FATHER "
320 DATA " DREAMS "," DREAM "
330 DATA " I "," YOU@ "," YOU "," I "," ME "," YOU "
340 DATA " MY "," YOUR* "
350 DATA " YOUR "," MY "," MYSELF "," YOURSELF* "
360 DATA " YOURSELF "," MYSELF "
370 DATA " I'M "," YOU'RE* "," YOU'RE "," I'M "," AM "," ARE@ "
380 DATA " WERE "," WAS "
390 NEXT PS, I
400 RETURN
410 '            Keyword processing
420 '            A. Checking for keywords
430 IF X = 1 THEN 900
440 FOR I = 1 TO NU
450 READ KE$, JU
460 FOR PS = 1 TO LEN(PA$) - LEN(KE$) + 1
470 IF KE$ = MID$(PA$, PS, LEN(KE$)) THEN DR$ =
    MID$(PA$, PS + LEN(KE$)): IF DR$ <> "" THEN 500 ELSE 900
480 NEXT PS, I
490 GOTO 790
```

101

```
500 DR$ = LEFT$(DR$, LEN(DR$) - 1): GOTO 900
510 DATA "COMPUTER",1,"MACHINE",1
520 DATA " NAME ",2,"ALIKE",3," LIKE ",3," SAME ",3
530 DATA "YOU@ REMEMBER",4,"DO I REMEMBER",5,"YOU@ DREAMED",6
540 DATA " DREAM ",7," IF ",8,"EVERYBODY",9,"EVERYONE",9
550 DATA "NOBODY",9,"NO ONE",9,"WAS YOU@",10,"YOU@ WAS",11
560 DATA "WAS I",12,"YOUR* MOTHER",13,"YOUR* FATHER",13
570 DATA "YOUR* SISTER",13,"YOUR* BROTHER",13,"YOUR* WIFE",13
580 DATA "YOUR* HUSBAND",13,"YOUR* CHILDREN",13,"YOUR*",14
590 DATA "ALWAYS",15,"ARE I",16,"ARE@ YOU@",18," HOW ", 25
600 DATA "BECAUSE",19,"CAN I",20,"CAN YOU@",21,"CERTAINLY",22
610 DATA "DEUTSCH",23,"ESPANOL",23,"FRANCAIS",23,"HELLO",24
620 DATA "I REMIND YOU OF",3,"I ARE",26,"I'M",26
630 DATA "ITALIANO",23,"MAYBE",28," MY ",29," NO ",30
640 DATA "PERHAPS",28,"SORRY",31,"WHAT ",25,"WHEN ",25
650 DATA "WHY DON'T I",32,"WHY CAN'T YOU@",33,"YES",22
660 DATA "YOU@ WANT",34,"YOU@ NEED",34," ARE ",17," I ",27
670 DATA "YOU@ ARE@ SAD",35,"YOU'RE* SAD",35
680 DATA "YOU@ ARE@ UNHAPPY",35,"YOU'RE* UNHAPPY",35
690 DATA "YOU@ ARE@ DEPRESSED",35,"YOU'RE* DEPRESSED",35
700 DATA "YOU@ ARE@ SICK",35,"YOU'RE* SICK",35
710 DATA "YOU@ ARE@ HAPPY",36,"YOU'RE* HAPPY",36
720 DATA "YOU@ ARE@ ELATED",36,"YOU'RE* ELATED",36
730 DATA "YOU@ ARE@ GLAD",36,"YOU'RE* GLAD",36
740 DATA "YOU@ ARE@ BETTER",36,"YOU'RE* BETTER",36
750 DATA "YOU@ FEEL YOU@",37,"YOU@ THINK YOU@",37
760 DATA "YOU@ BELIEVE YOU@",37,"YOU@ WISH YOU@",37
770 DATA " YOU@ ARE@",38,"YOU'RE*",38,"YOU@ CAN'T",39
780 DATA "YOU@ CANNOT",39,"YOU@ DON'T",40,"YOU@ FEEL",41
790 '          B. No keywords found
800 IF YO$ = "" THEN 810 ELSE RAN = RND(5):
    ON RAN GOTO 810, 810, 810, 860, 860
810 RAN = RND(4): ON RAN GOTO 820, 830, 840, 850
820 PRINT "I AM NOT SURE I UNDERSTAND YOU FULLY.": X = 1:
    GOTO 900
830 PRINT "PLEASE GO ON.": X = 1: GOTO 900
840 PRINT "WHAT DOES THAT SUGGEST TO YOU?": X = 1: GOTO 900
850 PRINT "DO YOU FEEL STRONGLY ABOUT DISCUSSING SUCH THINGS?":
    X = 1: GOTO 900
860 RAN = RND(3): ON RAN GOTO 870, 880, 890
870 PRINT "LET'S DISCUSS FURTHER WHY YOUR" + YO$ + ".": X = 1:
    GOTO 900
880 PRINT "EARLIER YOU SAID YOUR" + YO$ + ".": X = 1: GOTO 900
890 PRINT
    "DOES THAT HAVE ANYTHING TO DO WITH THE FACT THAT YOUR" +
    YO$ + "?": X = 1: GOTO 900
900 RETURN
910 '          Marker remover
920 IF X = 1 THEN 960
930 FOR PS = 1 TO LEN(DR$)
940 IF MID$(DR$, PS, 1)= "@" OR MID$(DR$, PS, 1) = "*" THEN
    DR$ = LEFT$(DR$, PS - 1) + MID$(DR$, PS + 1)
950 NEXT PS
960 RETURN

970 '          Doctor's reply
980 '          A. Line to jump to
990 IF X = 1 THEN 1470
1000 ON JU GOTO 1020,1030,1040,1050,1060,1070,1080,1090,1100,
1110,1120,1130,1140,1150,1160,1170,1180,1190,1200,1210,1220,
1230,1240,1250,1260,1270,1280,1290,1300,1310,1320,1370,1380,
1390,1400,1410,1420,1430,1440,1450,1460
```

```
1010 '            B. Replies
1020 PRINT "DO COMPUTERS WORRY YOU?": GOTO 1470
1030 PRINT "I AM NOT INTERESTED IN NAMES.": GOTO 1470
1040 PRINT "IN WHAT WAY?": GOTO 1470
1050 PRINT "DO YOU OFTEN THINK OF" + DR$ + "?": GOTO 1470
1060 PRINT "DID YOU THINK I WOULD FORGET" + DR$ + "?":
     GOTO 1470
1070 PRINT "REALLY, " + DR$ + "?": GOTO 1470
1080 PRINT "WHAT DOES THAT DREAM SUGGEST TO YOU?": GOTO 1470
1090 PRINT "DO YOU THINK IT'S LIKELY THAT IF " + DR$ + "?":
     GOTO 1470
1100 PRINT "REALLY, " + KE$ + "?": GOTO 1470
1110 PRINT "WHAT IF YOU WERE" + DR$ + "?": GOTO 1470
1120 PRINT "WERE YOU REALLY?": GOTO 1470
1130 PRINT "WOULD YOU LIKE TO BELIEVE I WAS" + DR$ + "?":
     GOTO 1470
1140 PRINT "TELL ME MORE ABOUT YOUR FAMILY.": GOTO 1470
1150 PRINT "YOUR" + DR$ + ".": GOSUB 1480: GOTO 1470
1160 PRINT "CAN YOU THINK OF A SPECIFIC EXAMPLE?": GOTO 1470
1170 PRINT "WHY ARE YOU INTERESTED IN WHETHER I AM" + DR$ +
     " OR NOT?": GOTO 1470
1180 PRINT "DID YOU THINK THEY MIGHT NOT BE " + DR$ + "?":
     GOTO 1470
1190 PRINT "DO YOU BELIEVE YOU ARE" + DR$ + "?": GOTO 1470
1200 PRINT "IS THAT THE REAL REASON?": GOTO 1470
1210 PRINT "YOU BELIEVE I CAN" + DR$ + ", DON'T YOU?":
     GOTO 1470
1220 PRINT "WHETHER OR NOT YOU CAN" + DR$ +
     " DEPENDS ON YOU MORE THAN ON ME.": GOTO 1470
1230 PRINT "YOU SEEM QUITE POSITIVE.": GOTO 1470
1240 PRINT "I AM SORRY, I SPEAK ONLY ENGLISH.": GOTO 1470
1250 PRINT "HOW DO YOU DO.": GOTO 1470
1260 PRINT "WHY DO YOU ASK?": GOTO 1470
1270 PRINT "WHAT MAKES YOU THINK I AM" + DR$ + "?": GOTO 1470
1280 PRINT "WE WERE DISCUSSING YOU, NOT ME.": GOTO 1470
1290 PRINT "YOU DON'T SEEM QUITE CERTAIN.": GOTO 1470
1300 PRINT "WHY ARE YOU CONCERNED OVER MY " + DR$ + "?":
     GOTO 1470
1310 PRINT "ARE YOU SAYING 'NO' JUST TO BE NEGATIVE?":
     GOTO 1470
1320 RAN = RND(4): ON RAN GOTO 1330, 1340, 1350, 1360
1330 PRINT "PLEASE DON'T APOLOGIZE.": GOTO 1470
1340 PRINT "APOLOGIES ARE NOT NECESSARY.": GOTO 1470
1350 PRINT "WHAT FEELINGS DO YOU HAVE WHEN YOU APOLOGIZE?":
     GOTO 1470
1360 PRINT "YOU NEEDN'T FEEL THAT YOU HAVE TO APOLOGIZE.":
     GOTO 1470
1370 PRINT "DO YOU BELIEVE I DON'T" + DR$ + "?": GOTO 1470
1380 PRINT "DO YOU THINK YOU SHOULD BE ABLE TO" + DR$ +"?":
     GOTO 1470
1390 PRINT "WHAT WOULD IT MEAN TO YOU IF YOU GOT" + DR$ +"?":
     GOTO 1470
1400 GOSUB 1510: GOSUB 1540:
     PRINT "I AM SORRY TO HEAR YOU ARE" + DR$ + ".": GOTO 1470
1410 GOSUB 1510: GOSUB 1540:
     PRINT "HOW HAVE I HELPED YOU TO BE" + DR$ + "?": GOTO 1470
1420 PRINT "DO YOU REALLY THINK SO?": GOTO 1470
1430 PRINT "IS IT BECAUSE YOU ARE" + DR$ +
     " THAT YOU CAME TO ME?": GOTO 1470
1440 PRINT "HOW DO YOU KNOW YOU CAN'T" + DR$ + "?": GOTO 1470
1450 PRINT "DON'T YOU REALLY" + DR$ + "?": GOTO 1470
1460 PRINT "TELL ME MORE ABOUT SUCH FEELINGS.": GOTO 1470
1470 RETURN
```

```
1480 '          Special processing if keyword is MY
1490 IF LEN(DR$) > 11 THEN YO$ = DR$
1500 RETURN

1510 '          Remove "@" marker from key phrase if present
1520 IF MID$(KE$, 4, 1) = "@" THEN DR$ =
     RIGHT$(KE$, LEN(KE$) - 9)
1530 RETURN

1540 '          Remove "x" marker from key phrase if present
1550 IF MID$(KE$, 7, 1) = "x" THEN DR$ =
     RIGHT$(KE$, LEN(KE$) - 7)
1560 RETURN
```

Possible Modifications

(1) The keyword and reply routines can be augmented so that DOCTOR has a wider range of replies and can handle a more diverse set of situations than before. Conversely, these routines can be trimmed to help improve program speed.

(2) If your BASIC has no LINE INPUT statement, but does contain INKEY$, GET, or a similar keyboard-strobe function, you can rewrite the input routine so that sentences input to DOCTOR may include commas or other termination characters. During initialization, set up a one-dimensional, 100-element array PA$; this will hold the separate letters of the input sentence. After the character is gotten from the keyboard by INKEY$ (or GET), it is printed. Let a variable N contain the number of letters that the patient has typed in the course of entering the sentence. If the incoming character is a backspace, N = N − 1; if it is anything else, N = N + 1. Each time a letter (as opposed to a backspace) is typed, it is stored in the next available location in PA$ (e.g., PA$(N) = LETTER). If, however, the incoming character is a carriage return, a FOR. . .NEXT loop which cycles N times is activated. This FOR. . .NEXT loop concatenates all the individual elements of array PA$. The result is the complete input sentence, commas and all.

(3) There is no compelling reason why DOCTOR should be limited to psychotherapy. You might try transforming DOCTOR into a G.P. by programming it to respond with brief medical lectures to keywords like "ulcer" and "back pain." Or the doctor association could be abandoned completely and the program made to simulate the responses of, say, a salesman or a child.

Explanation of Special
BASIC Keywords

In an effort to make the programs in this book more easily translatable into the version of BASIC which the reader is accustomed to using, this appendix is supplied. It contains descriptions of the special BASIC keywords used in the programs which may not be included in the reader's BASIC, or may not have the same function.

Keywords whose functions seem to be relatively steady from BASIC to BASIC (e.g., PRINT, READ, GOTO, etc.) are not included. Only the portion of the keyword's attributes which is used in the book's programs (or mentioned in the text) is described.

BASIC Keyword	Description
CHR$(n)	Takes ASCII, control, or graphics code n and returns the associated character
DEFSNG v	Defines variable(s) v as single-precision
DEFSTR v	Defines variable(s) v as string type
INKEY$	Inputs a single character from the keyboard
LEN(s)	Returns number of characters in string s
LINE INPUT	Inputs a line of text from the keyboard. Not affected by commas or other termination characters. Carriage return ends input
LEFT$(s, n)	Returns the leftmost n characters of string s
MID$(s, p)	Returns the right-hand portion of string s beginning at position p
MID$(s, p, n)	Returns a substring of string s, beginning at position p, n characters long

PEEK(m)	Returns the byte which is stored in memory location m
POKE m, b	Puts byte b into memory location m
POS(d)	Returns a number which indicates the column in which the cursor is presently located. d is a dummy argument
PRINT @ n	Prints the item at a certain location n on the display
RANDOM	Resets the random-number generator RND so that different runs of the program cause RND to produce different sequences of random numbers
RIGHT$(s, n)	Returns the rightmost n characters of string s
RND(n)	Generates a random number between 1 and n
STR$(n)	Converts a number n to a string
STRING$(n, c)	Returns a variable-length string composed of a certain character c. c may be specified by giving the actual character or by using its ASCII code. The length of the string is determined by n
VAL(s)	Converts a string s to a number

Additionally, the type declaration character "$" is used to indicate that the variable preceding it is string type, while the operator "+" is used for string concatenation (as well as to indicate simple addition).

Index

TO THE READER

Sams Computer books cover Fundamentals — Programming — Interfacing — Technology written to meet the needs of computer engineers, professionals, scientists, technicians, students, educators, business owners, personal computerists and home hobbyists.

Our Tradition is to meet your needs and in so doing we invite you to tell us what your needs and interests are by completing the following:

1. I need books on the following topics:

_____

_____

_____

_____

_____

_____

2. I have the following Sams titles:

_____

_____

_____

_____

_____

_____

3. My occupation is:

_____ Scientist, Engineer	_____ D P Professional
_____ Personal computerist	_____ Business owner
_____ Technician, Serviceman	_____ Computer store owner
_____ Educator	_____ Home hobbyist
_____ Student	Other _____
	_____

Name (print) _____

Address _____

City _____ State _____ Zip _____

Mail to: **Howard W. Sams & Co., Inc.**
Marketing Dept. #CBS1/80
4300 W. 62nd St., P.O. Box 7092
Indianapolis, Indiana 46206